THE EXPECTANT FATHER'S
CRADLE BOAT BOOK

THE EXPECTANT FATHER'S
CRADLE BOAT BOOK

Text by Peter H. Spectre and Illustrations by Buckley Smith

WOODENBOAT PUBLICATIONS, INC. BROOKLIN, MAINE 04616

1990

Published by WoodenBoat Publications, Inc.
Naskeag Road
Brooklin, Maine 04616

Library of Congress Cataloging-in-Publication Data

Spectre, Peter H.
    The expectant father's cradle boat book / by Peter H. Spectre and
Buckley Smith.
        p.   cm.
    Includes bibliographical references.
    ISBN 0-937822-16-7 (softcover) : $14.95
    1. Furniture making. 2. Cradles. 3. Boatbuilding. I. Smith,
Buckley, 1947-   . II. Title.
TT197.5.C5S64 1990
684.1'5--dc20   90-12772
                                                                    CIP

Printed in the United States of America

OF CRAFTSMANSHIP
AND BOATS AND BABIES

A few years ago, at about 6:00 a.m. on a glorious summer day, I stopped for breakfast at Darre's Lunch in Belfast, Maine. Halfway through my first cup of coffee, Buck Smith, an artist and craftsman I hadn't seen for years, sat down next to me and—after the gee-look-who's-heres were finished—started telling me about a poster he was thinking about producing. It would consist of whimsical, stylized drawings and plans for building a little boat that could serve as a cradle. Buck had designed and built a rocking cradle boat for his 1½-year-old son Bowen back in 1982. It was a clever thing and could rock both fore-and-aft and athwartships. With his gift for invention and illustration, Buck could surely make such a poster work. But I wondered whether there might be something larger here. "Strange that you should mention that," I said. I, too, had been thinking about cradle boats—more specifically, about a little book on how to build them. The only thing holding

me back was art: The book I envisioned had to be illustrated with whimsical, stylized drawings and plans.... By the time I'd finished my second cup of coffee, Buck and I were in the cradle-boat-book business.

The true beginning of the project for me was back in 1983 when the editors of *WoodenBoat* magazine—of which I was one—received a package in the mail from Guy Hammon of McNeal, Arizona. Guy had been reading *The Dory Book* by John Gardner, which is a history of the dory and its several subspecies and includes boat plans and building instructions. Like many others who have been exposed to John Gardner's writings, Guy was inspired to build a boat, a wooden boat, a wooden boat that was simple in design and form but contained enough of those peculiar complexities of construction that make boatbuilding a slightly higher craft than, say, building a birdhouse or a bookcase. Boatbuilding, after all, involves skills not usually required in

straight carpentry and woodworking—curved shapes and complex geometry, for example, and odd bevels and tapers.

But Hammon had never built a boat before, and even though Gardner had laid out the principles of wooden boat building in an easily understood fashion, Hammon knew that reading and doing were two different things. He decided to start small. A model, perhaps, or a kid's boat.

The package we received contained a short article and a selection of color slides. Would *WoodenBoat* like to publish a story about Guy Hammon's first boatbuilding project? Actually, the article was about Guy's first cradle-building project. He hadn't built a boat model or a kid's boat, but a cradle in the shape of a boat, using the exact same techniques used in "normal" boatbuilding. Guy had built it for some friends who were expecting a baby. The slides showed the finished product: a beautiful little pram set on rockers, decorated with hearts cut out of the transoms (see page 57). Cute? I'd say so.

There wasn't a person on the *WoodenBoat* editorial staff who wasn't impressed with the concept and the quality of the workmanship. We had never seen anything like it. The cradle even had frames, just like a full-sized boat!

We all agreed that the builder had done a great job and the cradle embodied considerable original thinking and Guy Hammon ought to be congratulated, but the consensus was that the subject was a little too thin for a serious magazine whose major mission was the promotion and preservation of full-scale wooden boats. In those days our editorial direction was so pure that we even stayed away from model-boat construction.

But something about the combination of cradles and boats and babies struck a chord in me. A certifiable boat nut, a bona fide baby lover, a father who for the most part had felt left out of the pre-birth celebration of all three of my children no matter how many times I had been assured that I was part of the team, I couldn't help fantasizing about how wonderful it would be to build a cradle in the shape of a boat for a soon-to-be-born baby. While my wife was sitting by the fire in the living room knitting sweaters and booties, I'd be out in the shop hand-crafting a little boat that would gently rock my baby to sleep—a protective cocoon that I would build for my baby with love and care and attention to detail. Never mind that my children were teenagers by then and would have found a cradle about as useful as a maypole.

To my mind, this went to the heart of the concept of fatherhood. This had to do with love and its relationship to craftsmanship, craftsmanship and its relationship to fine boats, fine boats and their relationship to security of body and mind. If you could craft a fine boat, using the best materials and the most refined techniques, and the boat could protect your most cherished being—a baby—then that boat would become symbolic of your role as a father. Buck Smith had done it in what seemed to be an effortless manner. Almost in a spirit of play. If only we could encourage others to do the same.

High-minded notions, those, and difficult to express in the best of circumstances. In an editorial meeting... well, they probably sounded like the ravings of a sentimental lunatic. The editors viewed the matter with a more literal mind than mine: *WoodenBoat* was about boats that floated, and since Hammon's cradle boat wasn't designed to do that, then it didn't deserve to be in the magazine. Guy Hammon's article was rejected.

But not quite. As author of the magazine's news column, I was free to classify anything I wanted as news, and to my mind this was news. While the heartless troglodytes on the editorial staff went back to business as usual, I wrote a note to Guy Hammon and asked him if he would mind if I published a photograph of his cradle boat in the magazine's news column. Of course he wouldn't mind.

The photograph appeared in the May/June 1983 issue of *Wooden-Boat* with the following caption: "The lovely cradle boat. Can anyone top this?" Naturally, it was purely a rhetorical question. Guy, who had been working in a vacuum, thought he was the first person to build such a craft. Few others, including me, would have presumed to dispute such a claim. The idea was simply too original.

How wrong we were. Within days we started getting letters and photographs, even plans on occasion, from people who had built cradle boats or who owned them. From around the world! New construction and antiques! Cradles built as dories, skiffs, peapods, a Viking ship, prams, a sandbagger, a speedboat. There were cradle boats in museums, for goodness' sake. The grandson of the founder of Chris-Craft had been rocked to sleep in a cradle shaped like a runabout, for goodness' sake. There was no end to the variations. We had tapped into a heretofore-unchronicled underground movement.

Since then, *WoodenBoat*'s news column has contained usually one, sometimes more, photographs of the latest, best work in the cradle-boat field. Some of the boats have been plain, some have been fancy, some have been simple, some have embodied construction tech-niques that are at the pinnacle of wooden boat artistry; but all demonstrate an elemental truth: Love and crafts-manship go hand in hand.

Like cradle boats themselves, this is a small, uncom-plicated book. In it are a few examples of some of the best cradle boats that have been built to date, both an-tique and modern; thoughts on building techniques and the selection of tools and materials; complete building plans for two cradle boats specially designed for this book; and advice on adapting an existing full-sized boat design for cradle-boat construction.

If you can handle the basic woodworking tools and read directions, you'll find nothing difficult about building a cradle boat. All it takes is concentration and care, and a clear vision in your mind of the chubby-cheeked little baby who will some day take up residence in your creation. If that doesn't make you proud, I don't know what will.

—Peter H. Spectre
Camden, Maine, 1990

CONTENTS

CHAPTER ONE

SETTING UP SHOP

Finding space to build a cradle boat is not as difficult as it would seem. A large, fully outfitted shop would be nice, of course, but it is not necessary.

THE WORKSHOP

All that is really required is a small room, or the corner of a large room. A cellar, a garage, a porch, even the backyard will do. You only need space enough to set up your building jig—the temporary form on which the boat will be built—and store your tools and materials.

Many years ago I built a plywood sailing skiff, twice the size of a cradle boat, in a one-bedroom apartment. I made patterns for the plywood pieces in advance and cut them out in the parking lot the same day I brought the plywood sheets home from the lumberyard. When I wasn't working on the boat, I stored my tools and the smallest pieces in a closet, and slid the large pieces under the couch and the bed. I started working on the boat in the living room and actually planked it and fitted it out on the balcony. I had my problems, like not having enough room to stand back and sight the sheer to check it for fairness, but, all and all, everything worked out just fine. A boat the size of a baby's cradle, one that would have fit on the dining table, would have been simple by comparison.

If you are working during the cold-weather months, try to find a heated space. If you can't, at least bring the boat inside when you are gluing and painting; otherwise, things won't set up properly. A cradle boat, no matter what design you choose to build, is small and light enough to be easily moved from place to place. But remember, you will have to contend with paint, resin, and glue fumes, plus wood dust, some of which—to a greater or lesser extent, depending on the product—can be hazardous to your health and that of the mother- and baby-in-waiting. Pay attention to these things! Ventilate your workspace! Follow the instructions accompanying any of the products you use to the letter!

BUILDING BENCH

The building jig for either one of the cradle boats whose plans are provided in this book can be mounted on a stool, which makes moving and storing the entire setup quite easy. A sawhorse is even better, because it will provide more stability. The best type of sawhorse for the purpose (see Figure 1) has a wide top with plenty of surface for clamping the building jig and supporting large pieces of lumber while you saw them. Even better is a solidly fixed surface, such as a tablesaw, so the jig can be solidly secured.

FIGURE 1

A minimum tool kit for building the cradle boats shown in this book would include the following:

HAND SAW—crosscut, fine toothed

HAMMER

STEEL RULE

FRAMING SQUARE—to check accuracy when setting up the box beam and station molds for the Bahama dinghy

TAPE MEASURE

MARKING PENCIL

CARBON PAPER—for tracing patterns

SCREWDRIVERS—straight and Phillips head (for driving sheetrock screws)

DRILL AND BITS—hand or power

BLOCK PLANE

SABERSAW—fine blade for cutting plywood; medium blade for cutting boards

CHISELS—$1/4''$, $1/2''$, and larger

FAIRING BATTEN—$1/8'' \times 1/4'' \times 4'$, pine or spruce (if building the Bahama dinghy, use a spare planking strip)

PUTTY KNIFE

SQUEEGEE—small auto-body type for working with epoxy resin on the Bahama dinghy

PAINT ROLLER (high-density foam), ROLLER TRAY, and MIXING

CUPS—for fiberglassing the Bahama dinghy

DISPOSABLE BRISTLE BRUSHES (or make "brushes" out of strips of a high-density foam roller cover)—for fiberglassing the Bahama dinghy

CLAMPS—small (2") and medium (4"), the more the better

CARPENTER'S SLIDING BEVEL

DIVIDERS

SHARPENING STONES—coarse, medium, and fine

SANDPAPER—use production paper, 60 and 80 grit, painted boat; also 150 or 220 grit, varnished boat

MASKING TAPE OR DUCT TAPE

STAPLE GUN (hand powered)—for stapling the strip planks in the Bahama dinghy

STAPLE REMOVER—or use pliers, carefully

A more elaborate tool kit that would make the task substantially easier would include:

TABLE SAW—combination blade, plus a planer blade if you are building the Bahama dinghy

BANDSAW

JACK PLANE

THICKNESS PLANER

An awkward part of building either one of our cradle boats is sawing the plywood, especially if you have a small shop and no power tools. A 4' x 8' sheet of plywood can be a handful. Consider cutting the plywood into manageable pieces from which you can later cut the individual parts. This requires careful planning—you don't want to cut the plywood into pieces that are smaller than the parts of the boat!—but is well worth the effort. Many lumberyards will saw sheets of plywood into smaller panels according to your specifications. Failing that, you might be able to do it yourself at a local school's industrial arts shop. Most shop teachers understand these things.

Be sure that your edge tools are sharp at all times. Experienced boatbuilders and woodworkers will tell you that more mistakes are made with dull tools than with sharp ones.

Though screws are usually thought of as fastenings, not tools, sheetrock screws in various lengths are indispensable for the cradle-boat builder and should be a part of your tool kit. These screws, made of hardened steel, are rather thin for their length and have coarse threads and very sharp points. They are also brittle and can

break more easily under stress than bronze or stainless-steel screws. Unlike regular screws, they do not require a pilot hole or countersinking in soft woods (they can split hardwood just like any other screw) and are extremely easy to drive, either with a hand screwdriver or a power driver. They are especially useful for those who work alone, as you can hold the work in place with one hand and drive the screws with the other. Once you get used to sheetrock screws, you will find that you can use them as clamps to hold pieces temporarily. Keep in mind, however, that the screws may be temporary but the holes they make aren't. Only use sheetrock screws in places that later can be filled with putty.

Your safety equipment should include the following:

SAFETY GOGGLES/GLASSES—to wear while working with power tools, to protect your eyes from any wayward bits of wood; or while working with epoxy or polyester resin

DISPOSABLE GLOVES—to protect your hands from contact with epoxy or polyester resin

RESPIRATOR—the charcoal-filtered type that can handle organic vapors and mists, to wear while working with epoxy or polyester resin

DUST MASK—to wear while working with power tools, to minimize the amount of wood dust you'll breathe, and while sanding epoxy

PLEASE PAY SPECIAL ATTENTION TO THIS:

It is not unusual for people to become sensitized to epoxy. Be wary of any possible reaction. The most common symptom would be a rash resembling poison ivy. If you should develop any kind of rash, stop using the epoxy immediately. If this or any unusual symptom should persist, see your doctor.

Even if you are not sensitized to epoxy, it is an irritant, and you should work carefully around it. Do not splash the epoxy, provide adequate ventilation, and wear protective clothing and disposable gloves.

To save money, polyester resin can be used as a substitute for epoxy for the fiberglassing called for in the Bahama dinghy (there is no requirement for fiberglassing the pram). It will not bond to the wood as well, but this is a cradle, not a seagoing boat. And, of course, be as careful in working with polyester as with epoxy.

If you would like more information on shop safety, WoodenBoat has published two articles on the subject of shop safety that are well worth reading: "Boatyard Hazards," WB No. 79, and "Boatbuilder, Beware," WB No. 93. For information on obtaining copies, contact: Research Department, WoodenBoat, Box 78, Brooklin, ME 04616; 207–359–4651.

CHAPTER TWO
THE CRADLE PRAM

This pram is the type of craft sailors use as a tender for larger boats, such as for ferrying passengers to shore, carrying groceries and supplies, and engaging in general, all-around harbor work. The boat's origins are in Scandinavia, where clean, functional design has always been valued.

Unlike the Bahama dinghy in the next chapter, which has a pointed bow and a transom at the stern, the pram has transoms both at the bow and the stern. This design increases carrying capacity and simplifies construction—ideal characteristics for a cradle. Wide and with a low center of gravity, the cradle pram is stable.

This is an uncomplicated design requiring materials readily available in the typical lumberyard. The building procedure is the essence of simplicity, since all parts can be cut from plans provided in this book. With the aid of a building jig, part of which will remain in the finished boat, the transoms, sides, bottom, frames, rails, floorboard, and rockers are shaped and assembled in a logical sequence. Glued and screwed together according to the accompanying instructions, the completed boat is ready to be painted and decorated to your taste.

The list of materials below is intended as a guideline only. Cradle boats are not built for the water, so there is no need to use marine-grade plywood, glue, paint, fastenings, or anything else so labeled. In fact, because the crew may attempt to eat the boat, it is imperative that you use non-toxic materials.

Many marine glues and paints are toxic. If you have any

doubts about the toxicity of the materials you might be using, ask your retailer or manufacturer to provide you with the most recent Material Safety Data Sheets. These contain information on the hazardous ingredients of the product, the potential hazards to your health, how to clean up spills, how to protect yourself while using the product, and special emergency first-aid procedures. Ask for the sheets—they must be provided by law—and keep them on file in your shop. If your supplier doesn't have them on hand, remind him of his obligation.

While many finishes may not be suitable for use on wooden toys or children's furniture, there are finishes that are formulated for such use. They include certain polyurethanes, and certain lacquers, varnishes, and oils. Hardware and paint stores should be able to provide complete information on non-toxic finishes. Also, several manufacturers of non-toxic finishes are listed in the Appendix. For further information, you might wish to inquire of the Consumer Products Safety Commission, Washington, DC 20207.

PLYWOOD

As it turns out, the cheapest plywood, so-called "doorskin plywood," approximately $1/8''$ thick, is the best for building the pram if economy is a consideration. More uniform than standard fir plywood, without knotholes and huge interior voids, it has surface plies of Philippine mahogany, which looks good when it is varnished and takes paint well. Of course, such plywood isn't the recommended $1/4''$ (see page 9), but it is nevertheless strong enough for the job.

If economy isn't a great consideration, there are many types of plywood that will produce a handsome cradle boat. Some, for example, have face veneers of exotic wood species, such as teak, African or Honduras mahogany, and walnut, and look lovely when finished bright with varnish. Most of those plywoods aren't available at the local lumberyard in $1/8''$ thickness (which for this type of plywood is easiest to bend), and will therefore have to be ordered specially. See the Appendix for a list of suppliers.

SOLID WOOD

Solid, natural lumber is required for the transoms, rubrails (gunwales), rockers, and trim. Almost any species that captures your fancy is suitable, though some are inappropriate where bending stock is called for, such as the rails. The best bending hardwoods are oak and ash; the best softwoods are spruce, pine, cedar, and poplar. Wood for bending should be straight-grained and free from knots. A few knots are acceptable in wood that will not be bent, but make sure they are tight, not loose and therefore liable to pop out.

If you should choose a hardwood for the rails, you may discover that it is too stiff to take the severe curve along the sheer. One solution to this problem would be to soak the rails overnight in the bathtub or, if you have access to a steambox, steam them for about 15 minutes. Another solution is to laminate the rails from two or three layers of thinner stock. If the latter, do the job right on the boat to achieve the proper curve. Lay the first strip on waxed paper to keep it from sticking to the boat, brush on glue, lay on the next layer, and clamp at close intervals along the length of the rail. After the glue has set up, remove the rail, sand it carefully, and fasten it permanently in place.

GLUE

The pram has been designed to use easily available,

inexpensive materials. Since it will not be put in the water, whether the glue you use is rated as waterproof or not is immaterial; you are free to use any type that will bond wood to wood, but in the interest of safety, be sure to use a type of glue that is non-toxic after it cures. (Check the label on the container for advice on toxicity; if you still have questions, ask your supplier to provide you with a copy of the Material Safety Data Sheet concerning the product.) The easiest to use is so-called carpenter's glue, such as Franklin's Titebond. Elmer's white glue will bond wood-to-wood joints, but it is not as strong as carpenter's glue. Carpenter's glue is inexpensive, doesn't require mixing, produces a joint as strong as the wood it bonds, and, since it is water soluble, is easily cleaned up

with a rag or sponge moistened with warm water.

Carpenter's glue is not gap-filling and therefore demands tight joints and careful clamping to be effective. If you have any doubts about being able to produce tight wood-to-wood joints, you might consider a two-part epoxy. Epoxy has the ability to fill gaps without losing strength and requires less clamping pressure. Its disadvantages are that it is messy to work with, relatively expensive, and can cause allergenic reactions for some users (see page 4).

Whatever type of glue you choose, be sure to follow the instructions on the label carefully, particularly regarding temperature. The best glue in the best joints can still fail if it is used outside the recommended temperature range. And clamp or fasten the joints tightly—the glue can hold only so much while it cures.

FASTENINGS

Marine-grade fastenings are not required for the pram. Nongalvanized common steel nails will work just fine, though you might consider using ring nails for their extra holding power. Steel screws and sheetrock screws are acceptable as well, though if you do not plan to putty over the heads, or bung them, you might consider brass or bronze screws for a fancier appearance.

FILLER, PAINT, AND VARNISH

Filler is required to cover countersunk fastenings and smooth out surface imperfections in the wood before finishing. Any of the various carpenter's nonshrinking wood fillers will do for surfaces that will be painted. Varnished surfaces require a filler that matches in color the wood to be filled.

For the best finish, all wood should be sealed before painting or varnishing. Varnished surfaces should be given a coat of clear sealer or at the least an initial coat of thinned varnish (approximately one-third paint thinner or turpentine to two-thirds varnish). If the wood contains knots, which tend to bleed through the finish, spot-prime the knots with shellac.

Painted surfaces should be sealed and primed. For this, use a dual-purpose product like BIN or Kilz.

Again, check the label on the container of any finish material you might use to be sure it is not toxic after it cures. Look up the Material Safety Data Sheet if you are uncertain.

LIST OF MATERIALS

PATTERNS

    Heavy builder's paper or thin cardboard

BUILDING JIG

    $3/4$" x $5 1/2$" x 32" spruce or pine boards, two pieces

    $3/4$" x 2" x 24" spruce or pine boards, two pieces

    $3/4$" x $5 1/2$" x 8" spruce or pine boards, three pieces

    $3/4$" x 1" x 10" spruce or pine transom alignment
        cleats, four pieces

BOW AND STERN TRANSOMS

    $3/4$" x 12" x 18" pine, mahogany, or oak boards, or other
        hardwood of your choice, two pieces

    (Note: If you cannot find acceptable stock as wide
        as 12", you can edge-glue two narrower boards.
        Do this on a flat surface, with waxed paper under
        the joint.)

SIDES, BOTTOM, AND FLOORBOARD

    $1/4$" Philippine mahogany plywood (also known as lauan
        plywood), one 4' x 8' sheet

    (Note: Furniture-grade plywood, such as mahogany,
        birch, etc., can be used. Since such plywood tends
        to be stiffer and therefore more difficult to bend,
        use $1/8$" stock.)

RUBRAILS (GUNWALES)

    $1/2$" x 36" pine half-round molding, two pieces (see
        also "Solid Wood," pages 6–7)

ROCKERS

    $3/4$" x $7 1/2$" x 25" pine, mahogany, or oak boards, or
        other hardwood of your choice, two pieces

FASTENINGS AND GLUE

    1" box nails ($1/2$ lb.)

    1" sheetrock screws ($1/2$ lb.)

    1" ring nails ($1/2$ lb.)

    Carpenter's glue

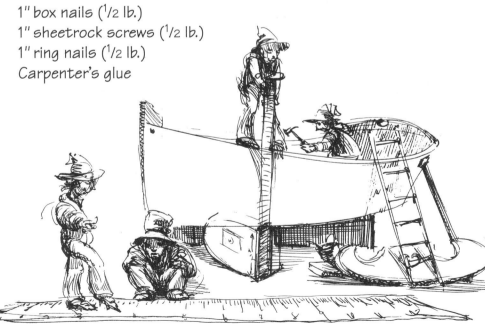

FIGURE 2

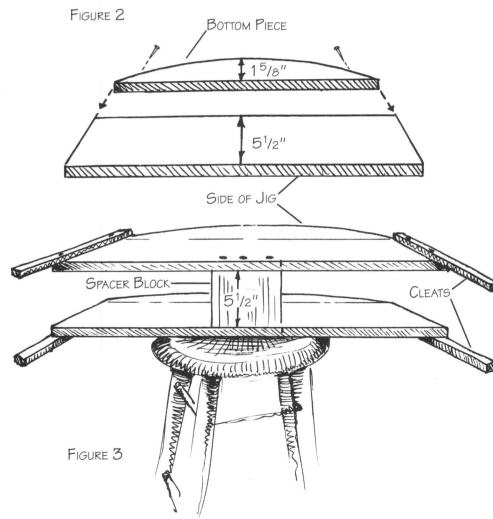

Bottom Piece

$1^{5}/8$"

$5^{1}/2$"

Side of Jig

Spacer Block

$5^{1}/2$"

Cleats

FIGURE 3

STEP-BY-STEP INSTRUCTIONS
STEP 1—MAKE THE PATTERNS

The pram plans (see pages 76–79), which have been reduced for reproduction in the book, must be redrawn to full size, enlarged to full size (600%) as described on page 34, or purchased (see page 75). To redraw to full size: For each pattern, lay off a grid-work of 1" squares on a sheet of heavy builder's paper or light cardboard. This grid represents a 600% increase from the page. Using the grid as a guide, transfer the pattern lines from the book to the builder's paper.

With scissors, cut out the patterns and label them.

STEP 2—BUILD THE JIG

Lay one $^3/4$" x $5^{1}/2$" x 32" spruce or pine board on top of the other, and either clamp or nail them temporarily together.

Lay down the pattern for the side pieces of the jig, tack it temporarily in place, and trace around it.

Remove the pattern and cut the boards to shape with a hand bow saw, a sabersaw, or a bandsaw.

Separate the pieces, being sure to mark which end is

the bow and which is the stern, for future reference.

Using two $3/4" \times 2" \times 24"$ spruce or pine boards, follow the same procedure to make the curved bottom pieces of the jig. Tack them to the bottoms of the side pieces with 1" box or finish nails. (Figure 2 shows how these pieces fit together.) The curved bottom pieces, which start out as part of the jig, will eventually become part of the structure of the boat, serving as bearers for the floorboard.

Nail the four $3/4" \times 1" \times 10"$ transom alignment cleats along the edges of the bow and stern ends of the side pieces. Use 1" box nails. These will provide proper support for mounting the transoms on the jig. With a chisel, trim off the outer corner at the top of each cleat, so the sides will fit properly over them.

Make the three spacer blocks as shown on the plans. Mark centerlines on the two blocks that will be aligned with the curved bottom of the jig. Starting with the middle spacer, nail all three blocks in place as indicated on the plans, by driving box nails through the side pieces into the end grain of the spacer blocks. (Figures 3 and 4 show the spacer blocks in place.)

The side pieces should now be parallel to each other and square with the spacer blocks. The building jig is now complete.

Clamp the jig to a stool, or to a sawhorse, or to a block of wood mounted on your workbench. The clamp should be positioned so it holds the middle spacer block tightly to the clamping surface. (In Figure 4 the clamp is obscured by the sides of the jig.)

Step 3—Make the Bow and Stern Transoms

These instructions apply equally to the bow and the stern transoms. To avoid confusion, first mark and cut one, and then the other.

Lay the transom pattern on the $3/4" \times 12" \times 18"$ board, such that the bottom edge of the pattern is aligned with the bottom edge of the board. Trace around the pattern, and transfer the centerline, indicated on the pattern, to the stock.

Cut out the transom, using a handsaw or portable circular saw to make the straight cuts and a bandsaw or sabersaw to make the curved top. (If you use a handsaw, a ripsaw will cut fast along the grain, while a crosscut saw will work best across the grain.)

Using a hand plane and a carpenter's bevel set to the

FIGURE 4

SPACER BLOCK

SPACER BLOCK

TRANSOM

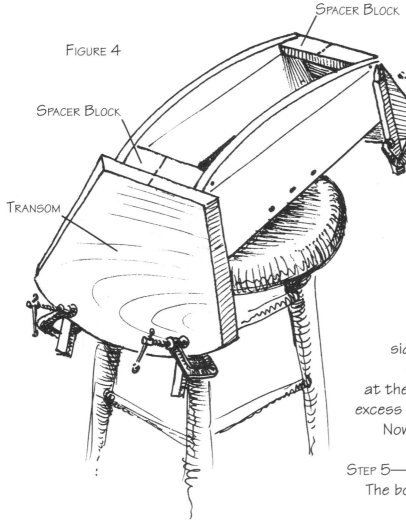

angles shown on the plans, bevel the bottom and side edges of the transom. Leave the curved top square for the time being. It will be beveled after the hull has been built.

Label the inside and the outside of the transom, and whether it is the bow or the stern, to avoid confusion later.

Now follow the same procedures for the other transom.

STEP 4 — MAKE THE SIDES

These instructions apply equally to both side panels of the boat. Lay the pattern on the plywood. If you are using $1/4''$ plywood, position the pattern so the face grain runs vertically. If you are using $1/8''$ plywood, which is easier to bend, you can position the pattern so the grain runs lengthwise.

Trace around the pattern and carefully mark which end is the bow and which is the stern, so you will know which way to mount the sides on the building jig.

Cut out the side. Saw right to the line at the sheer, within $1/4''$ or so at the bow and the chine, and within a couple of inches at the stern. This excess will be trimmed later.

Now follow the same procedures for the other side panel.

STEP 5 — MAKE THE BOTTOM

The bottom of the pram is made up of two layers of plywood cut to shape from the same pattern. Referring to the pattern, mark the centerline on each piece.

FIGURE 5

Cut out the bottom panels, leaving an extra margin of $1/4$" or so all the way around. This will be trimmed off later. (Avoid the temptation to cut right to the line; you may need this margin in order to bevel the bottom to receive the sides.)

STEP 6—MOUNT THE TRANSOMS ON THE JIG

If the transoms are to be painted, they can be fastened to the building jig with sheetrock screws. These can be removed later and the holes filled with carpenter's putty. If the transoms are to be varnished, they can be temporarily mounted on the building jig with clamps.

Position each transom at the appropriate end of the jig— the bow transom at the bow end, the stern transom at the stern end.

Align the transoms as shown in Figure 4. Be certain that their centerlines match the center of the jig. Check the positioning carefully.

Temporarily fasten the transoms to the four cleats on the jig. If you use sheetrock screws, drive them from the outside of the transoms into the cleats.

STEP 7—FASTEN THE TWO-LAYER BOTTOM TO THE JIG

Check that the curve of the bottom of the jig fairs into the bottom bevels of the transoms (see Figure 5), such that the jig-to-transom plane is continuous.

13

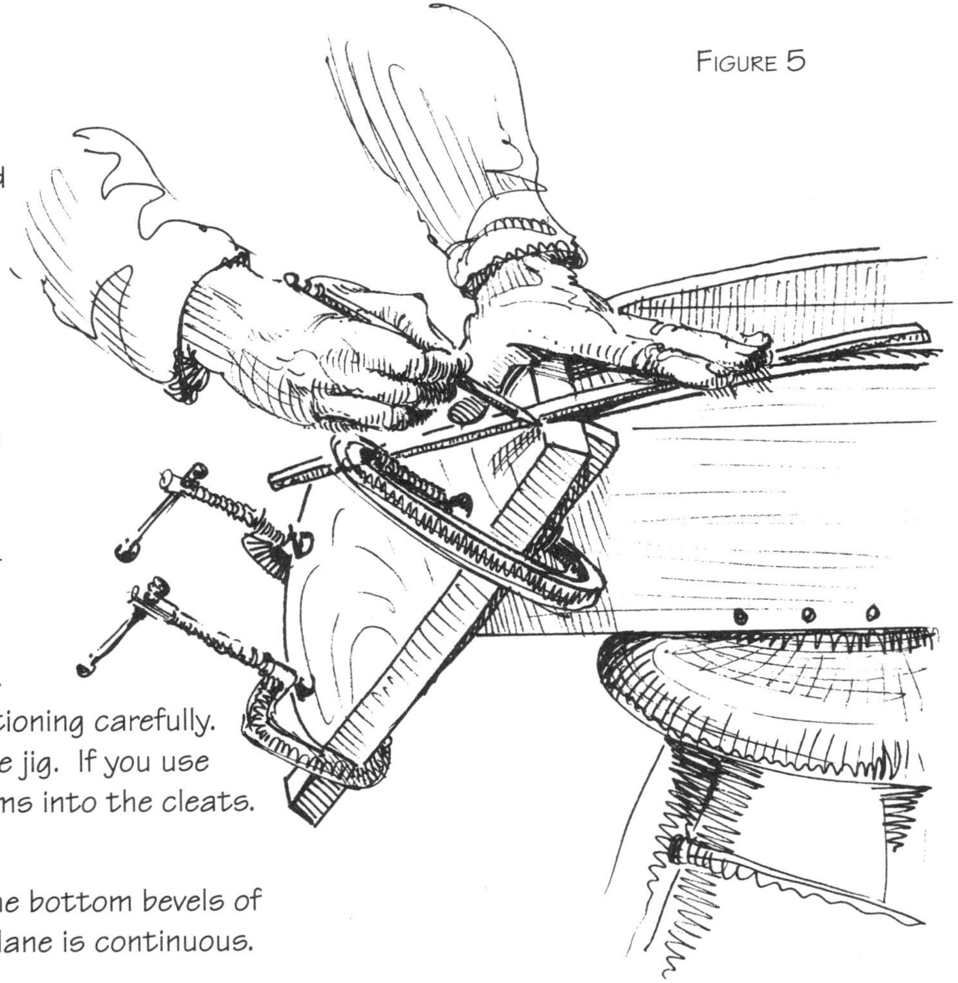

FIGURE 6

BOTTOM
(TWO LAYERS)

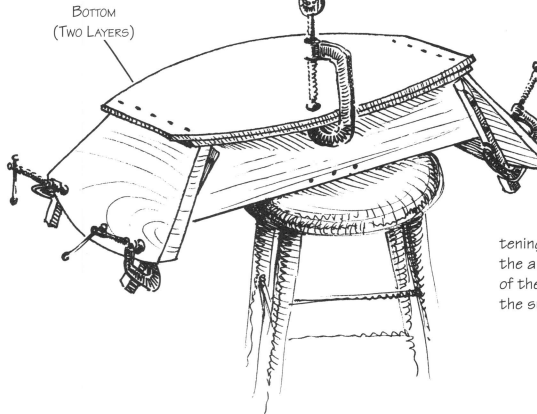

If it is not, plane the bevels until it is.

Spread glue (see page 7) on the bottom edges of the transoms, then line up the centerline of the first bottom piece with the centerlines of the transoms.

Fasten the ends of the bottom to the transoms, driving sheetrock screws or ring nails into the transoms, starting at the centerline and working toward the corners. Space the fastenings about 1" to 2" apart. Be careful to drive them at the angle of the transom so they don't run out the face of the transom. Make sure the fastenings are flush with the surface of the bottom, or are slightly countersunk.

FIGURE 7

Following the same procedures, glue and fasten the second bottom layer on top of the first (see Figure 6). Spread the glue on both surfaces, using a disposable paintbrush or a wide spreader stick. Clamp the layers around the edges while the glue sets up. The drawing shows one clamp, but it is better to use several. Use C-clamps, spring clamps, or old-fashioned one-piece clothespins.

When the glue has dried, hand plane the edges of the bottom so it fairs into the side bevels on the transoms (see Figure 7). Check for accuracy by springing a thin batten or one of the side pieces around the edges.

Finally, trim the bow and stern ends of the bottom in

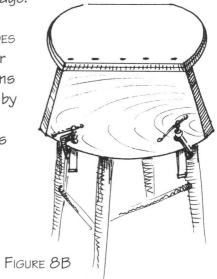

FIGURE 8A

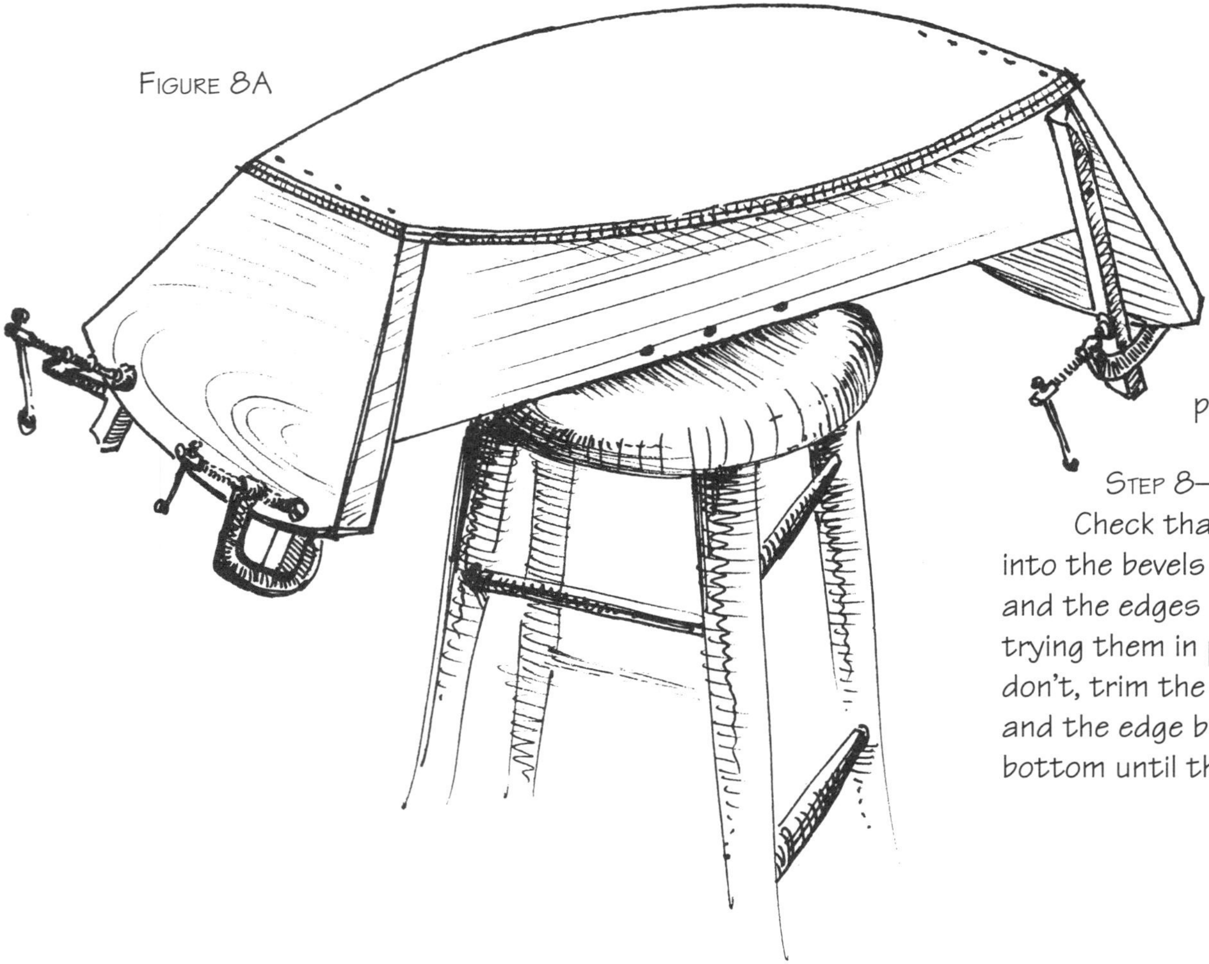

alignment with the transoms, and plane each end until it is fair with its corresponding transom. Figure 8 shows both side (A) and end (B) views of the cradle pram at this stage.

STEP 8—ATTACH THE SIDES
Check that the sides fair into the bevels of the transoms and the edges of the bottom by trying them in place. If they don't, trim the transom bevels and the edge bevels of the bottom until they do. Figures

FIGURE 8B

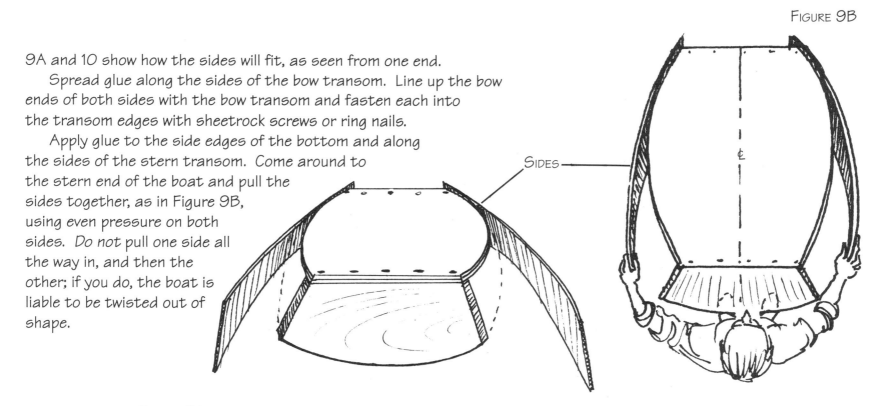

9A and 10 show how the sides will fit, as seen from one end.

Spread glue along the sides of the bow transom. Line up the bow ends of both sides with the bow transom and fasten each into the transom edges with sheetrock screws or ring nails.

Apply glue to the side edges of the bottom and along the sides of the stern transom. Come around to the stern end of the boat and pull the sides together, as in Figure 9B, using even pressure on both sides. Do not pull one side all the way in, and then the other; if you do, the boat is liable to be twisted out of shape.

SIDES

FIGURE 9B

FIGURE 9A

FIGURE 10

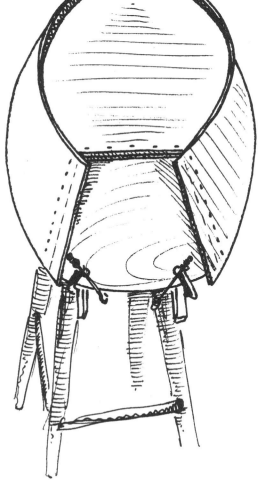

Glue and screw or nail the sides in place. Use light line to hold both sides in place while you fasten them, or lock your knee over one side while you fasten the other. (A helper here will simplify matters.) Figure 10 shows the sides glued and screwed in place.

Step 9—Trim the Sides

With a sharp handsaw, carefully trim off most of the excess plywood from the sides of the pram at the bow and the stern, as shown in Figure 11. Finish up with a block plane.

With a saw and a block plane, trim the excess plywood from the sides along the curve of the bottom.

At this point, the tops of the transoms will rise above the sheer (the tops of the sides). The excess here will be trimmed off later.

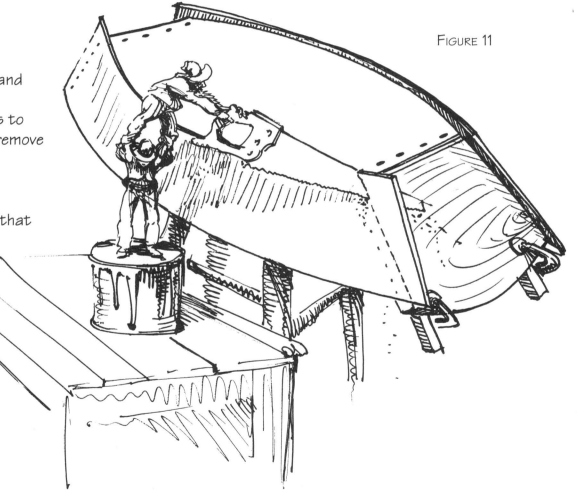

FIGURE 11

STEP 10—REMOVE THE BOAT FROM THE JIG

Unclamp the jig from the stool or workbench and turn the boat right-side up.

Depending on how you fastened the transoms to the jig, either back out the sheetrock screws or remove the clamps.

STEP 11—INSTALL THE FLOORBOARD BEARERS

The floorboard bearers are the curved pieces that were nailed to the bottom of the building jig. Pull the nails to remove them from the jig.

Lay the bearers in their proper position in the bottom of the boat and mark their locations. Remove them.

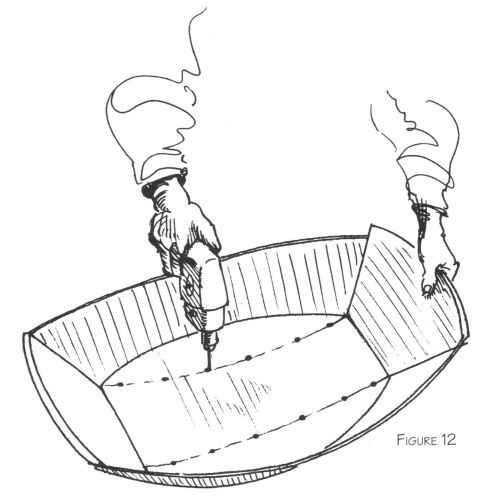

FIGURE 12

As shown in Figure 12, drill pilot holes through from the inside of the bottom where the bearers will lie.

Holding the bearers securely in position, drive sheet-rock screws from the outside through the bottom of the boat into the floorboard bearers. Figure 13 shows the floorboard bearers in place.

STEP 12—BEVEL THE TOPS OF THE TRANSOMS

With a plane, bevel the tops of the transoms so they fair into the sides (see Figure 14). Check your work carefully as you go to retain the proper curve.

FIGURE 13

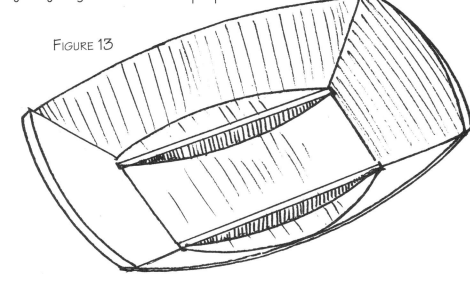

Step 13—Install the Rubrails (Gunwales)

If you are using two pieces of $\frac{1}{2}''$ half-round molding for the rails, fasten them along the sheer. It is best to allow them to run past the ends of the transoms and trim them later. Apply glue to the back of the rails, hold them in place with plenty of clamps, and screw the ends through the sides into the edges of the transoms. Pre-drill the rails for the screws to avoid splitting the wood.

If you are laminating the rails from thinner stock, follow the instructions on pages 6–7 under "Solid Wood."

Figure 14

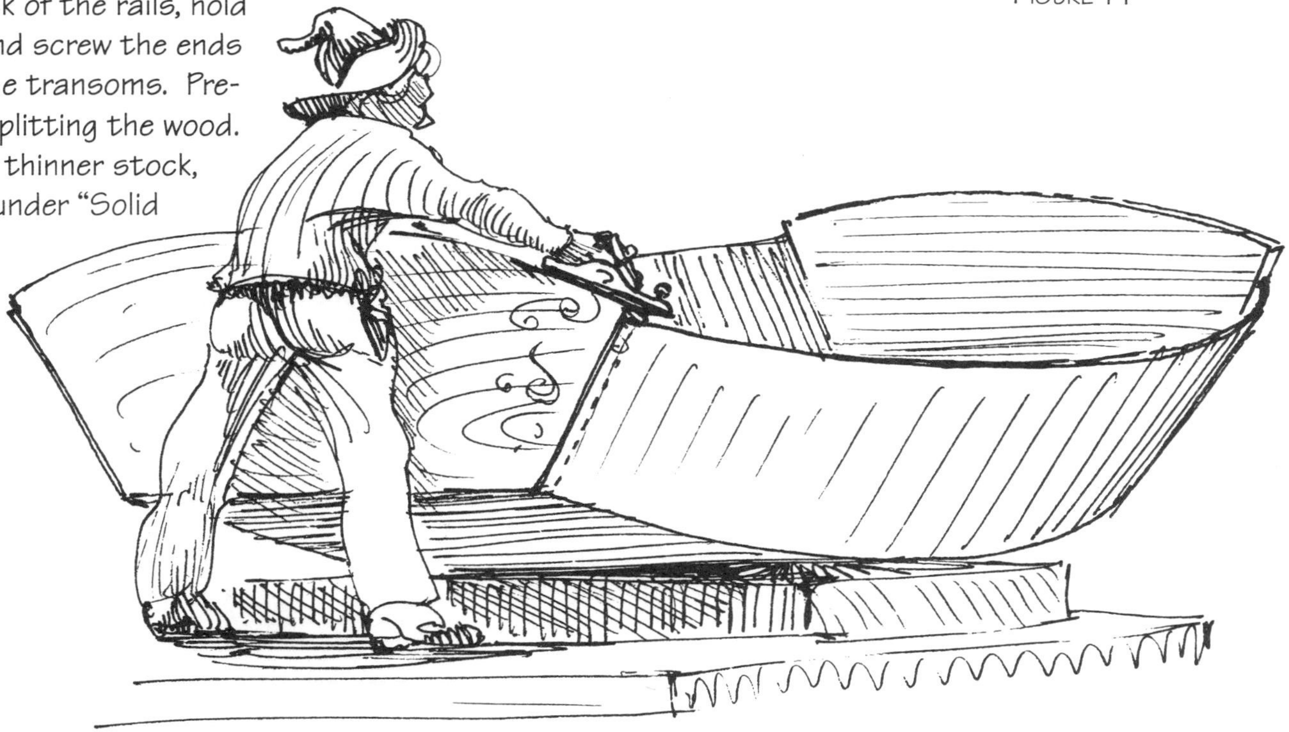

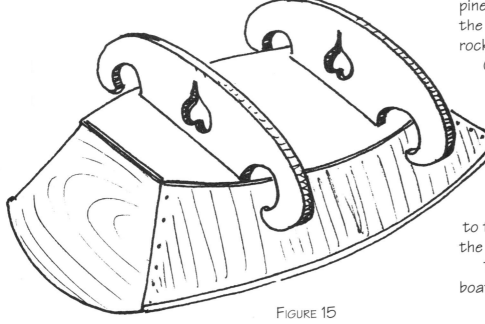

FIGURE 15

STEP 14—MAKE AND INSTALL THE ROCKERS

Place the rocker pattern of your choice (there are two shown on the plans) on a piece of $^3/4" \times 7^1/2" \times 25"$ pine, mahogany, oak, or other hardwood. Trace around the pattern, and repeat the process for the second rocker.

Cut out the rockers with a bandsaw or sabersaw. Finish the curved edges with a woodworker's file or rasp, followed by sandpaper. (If you should decide to decorate the rockers with cutout hearts, like those shown in Figure 15, or another design, drill a large pilot hole for the blade of your keyhole or sabersaw, then cut out the design.)

Locate the positions of the rockers according to the plans, and drill pilot holes through the bottom of the boat for the screws.

The rockers can be mounted to the bottom of the boat so they are parallel to each other and 90 degrees

22

to the floor, or flared out slightly at each end. It's your
choice. In either case, bevel the edges of the rockers so
they will bear against the bottom as you wish, and then
fasten them in place with sheetrock screws driven
through the bottom from the inside. Two or three screws
into each rocker will be fine.

STEP 15—INSTALL THE FLOORBOARD

Check to be sure the floorboard pattern fits properly
in the boat. If it does not, trim the pattern, then place
it on a piece of plywood, and trace around it.

Cut out the floorboard and fasten it in place by driving sheetrock screws down into the floorboard bearers,
as shown in Figure 16.

STEP 16—PAINT AND DECORATE THE BOAT

If there are any remaining holes, imperfections, or
countersunk screw heads to cover, now is the time to

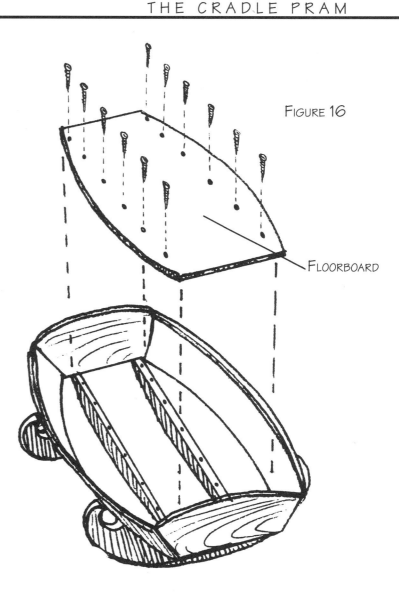

FIGURE 16

FLOORBOARD

23

apply the putty or other filler to smooth these out. Some of these may require a second application, due to the shrinkage of the filler. Keep in mind that imperfections tend to show up more when the finish is glossy, so work accordingly.

Sand the boat, then seal the wood with a clear sealer if the cradle is to be finished bright or a pigmented sealer if it is to be painted. Sand lightly once more. Again, in the interest of the health of your baby, be certain to use non-toxic finishes for this boat.

Varnish, paint, decorate, or embellish to your heart's content. You may even want to carve a name, the year, or other decoration into one or both of the transoms. As the drawing at right shows, you could even add a rudder.

You can make a little mattress from foam rubber or cotton batting and cover it with a fabric to suit. Beware only of making it too thick, which will raise the center of gravity of the cradle. One-inch foam, for example, is probably fine. Three-inch foam would be unnecessarily thick.

CHAPTER THREE

THE BAHAMA DINGHY

The Bahama dinghy is a round-bottomed boat used by the fishermen and traders of the Bahamas. It is noted for its sturdy construction, similarity to much larger island vessels, and large capacity for such a small craft. The typical dinghy is between 10 and 15 feet long, and is powered by a single leg-o'-mutton sail, a small outboard motor, or a single sculling oar. It is a general-purpose island boat used for sponging, tending fish traps, ferrying cargo from ship to shore, and as a tender to larger native craft. The lines of the Bahama dinghy shown here were taken off an existing boat and altered only slightly for a cradle.

In comparison to the pram discussed in the previous chapter, the Bahama dinghy is a more shapely design and is consequently more difficult and more time-consuming to build. If you have never built a boat before, you will find the construction of this one a challenge. The result, however, is a charming little cradle boat that is as salty as the sea.

The construction method used is what is known as strip planking, a modern technique used for building canoes and other craft. The hull is built upside down. Temporary molds are set up on a portable box beam, and long, thin strips of wood are bent around the molds and bonded edge-to-edge to make the skin of the boat. The resulting hull is strong enough to hold its shape without interior framing.

The materials required for the Bahama dinghy are more expensive than those for the pram, but if you follow the recommendations, you will be rewarded by an elegant craft that will live up to the time and expense involved in building it.

PLYWOOD

With the exception of the floorboard piece (if you build it of plywood), all of the plywood used in the Bahama dinghy is for the building jig—the box beam and the molds—and will not remain in the boat. Any type of

$1/2$" plywood will be fine, but it should be good-quality stock without voids, or with as few voids as possible. The last thing you want is a void just where you need solid wood for fastening down a strip plank.

You could economize by building the box beam out of particleboard. However, since particleboard doesn't cut as cleanly as plywood or hold fastenings as well and is not as rigid, it is best to use plywood for the molds.

SOLID WOOD

The best lumber for the planking strips is a softwood such as (in order of preference) pine, Eastern white cedar, spruce, Western red cedar, and redwood. Hardwood can be used, but since it tends to be stiffer than softwood, it is more difficult to bend around the severe curves of this hull, especially oak, which is also more difficult to bond with epoxy. If you should choose a hardwood, you will have to use thinner strips to make it bend properly. Whatever you use, be certain to choose stock that is free of knots and other imperfections, and has reasonably straight grain, since defects, in addition to ruining the good looks of your boat, will prevent the strips from bending in a fair curve. Lumberyards grade

such stock as "Select," but do not take their word for it. Inspect the lumber carefully. If you will be finishing the wood "bright," reject lumber with stains and other cosmetic imperfections.

The planking stock should be moderately dry to minimize shrinking and checking. Avoid kiln-dried lumber, however, as it tends to be stiff and brittle.

Most builders will want to use a hardwood such as mahogany, cherry, oak, or walnut for the transom, outer stem, rubrails, and knees.

As in the pram, the curve of the sheer is severe enough to make bending hardwood rails quite difficult. If bending solid pieces is impossible, you can laminate your rails from two thin pieces bent, glued, and clamped to the curve of the jig.

ADHESIVE

The best adhesive for this boat is epoxy, both for its strength and, when thickened, its gap-filling capabilities. The latter is especially important, since it is nearly impossible to obtain absolutely tight, wood-to-wood joints in strip planking.

Several of the two-part epoxies formulated for woodworking are suitable, but be sure to choose a brand that will give you sufficient working time (pot life) before it sets up (15 minutes is fine). If you cannot find an appropriate epoxy in your local hardware store or marine chandlery, see the list of suppliers in the Appendix.

Some epoxy manufacturers also sell inexpensive, reusable dispensing pumps that screw into the resin and hardener containers and dispense the proper ratio of resin to hardener with little waste or mess.

To give the epoxy its gap-filling characteristics, you'll want to thicken the resin/hardener mixture with a filler additive, such as colloidal silica or microballoons. The filler should be added to the thoroughly mixed resin/hardener until it reaches a peanut butter texture.

Most epoxy manufacturers provide detailed product-use instructions. To repeat a previous lecture, please be aware of the potential health hazards when using epoxy. Read the packaging instructions carefully, and follow them religiously. Provide adequate ventilation when mixing and applying epoxy, and wear disposable gloves and protective clothing. Use a respirator when sanding epoxy, and stop working immediately if you become sensitized.

Reasonable alternatives to epoxy are Elmer's carpenter's glue and Titebond, both of which are available in plastic squeeze bottles. They are less messy to use than epoxy, but they are not as strong and are not gap-filling, and require significantly more clamping pressure while curing.

FIBERGLASS CLOTH

Strip planking produces a very thin hull that relies on the strength of the epoxy joints and a fiberglass skin to hold it together. If the joints contain any epoxy-starved spots, there could be weaknesses in the hull itself. There could also be stresses in the hull brought on by changes in temperature during and after construction. By covering the outside of the hull with a layer of

fiberglass set in epoxy, these weaknesses and stresses will be compensated for. (An additional advantage to a well-saturated fiberglass covering is that it provides a very good underlayment for the final finish, whether it is paint or varnish.)

One layer of fine fiberglass cloth—4-ounce, or even 2-ounce, if you can find it—will be sufficient. The same epoxy that you used for the adhesive can often be used for bonding fiberglass cloth—check the manufacturer's recommendations. The same outlets that carry epoxy usually also stock compatible fiber-glass cloth.

For those who would pre-fer to avoid excessive use of synthetics, it should be noted that this cradle boat can be built with-out the layer of fiber-glass cloth set in epoxy. Many builders wouldn't recommend leaving off the 'glass, however, because

without it the hull would be more vulnerable to stress from moisture and temperature variations, and it would be more difficult to finish smooth.

FASTENINGS

Screws are required for constructing the building jig. Standard steel screws are fine for this purpose; sheet-rock screws are even better.

Steel screws can also be used in the boat itself—for example, to fasten the rails and the knees. However, since this cradle is actually a boat, it might be nice to add a more authentic touch with bronze or brass screws.

Staples, small screws, and some fine nails (4-penny or smaller common nails) are required to hold the plank-ing strips temporarily to the molds while the glue sets. Since holding power is of the highest concern, use $9/16''$ staples. A standard heavy-duty staple gun—Arrow is the principal brand name—is required.

FILLER, PAINT, AND VARNISH

The best filler for this boat is epoxy thickened with either microballoons or Gougeon's Microlight. Both are much easier to sand than a colloidal silica mixture, and yet offer plenty of strength.

After assembly and before painting or varnishing, all surfaces should be sealed with several coats of epoxy. The epoxy coatings can be applied one after another, without letting the epoxy cure. However, if the epoxy is allowed to cure overnight, the surface should be washed with clean water and plain paper towels to remove any amine blush, a water-soluble by-product of the epoxy curing process. After the final epoxy coat has cured, sand high spots smooth with fine-grit sandpaper before painting or varnishing.

Some epoxy-coated surfaces should be protected with paint or a varnish with ultraviolet-light inhibitors in its formulation. Be sure that all paint and varnish applied to your cradle is compatible with the brand of epoxy you're using. Before giving the cradle boat its final coat, test the compatibility in a small, inconspicuous area, or on a piece of scrap wood coated with epoxy.

In consideration of the health of the baby who will sleep in your boat, do not fail to check the label on the container of any finish material you might use to be sure it is not toxic after it cures. Look up the Material Safety Data Sheet if you are uncertain.

LIST OF MATERIALS

PATTERNS

To create the patterns, it is easiest to trace full-sized plans directly onto the wood. For this, you'll need a sheet of carbon paper and a set of the full-sized plans (see the Appendix, "Cradle Boat Plans").

You can enlarge the plans in this book (see pages 80–83), using a photocopier, and trace them through carbon paper onto the wood. If you should do this, be sure to enlarge them to the right scale, as described in Step 1, page 34.

Another method is to enlarge the plans by the grid method, redrawing them on heavy builder's paper or thin cardboard, and cut them out as full-sized patterns or templates, as described on page 10.

BOX BEAM

The box beam forms the base of the building jig. You can build it and the other parts of the building jig (molds, transom spacers, cleats, and stiffeners) all from one sheet of $1/2''$ plywood (4' x 8').

MOLDS, TRANSOM SPACERS, CLEATS, STIFFENERS, AND SPREADER

$1/2''$ plywood, cut from the same sheet as the box beam. There are nine molds in all (including the stem mold, which is cut from the same piece as the inner stem pattern, and the transom mold), two transom spacers, and two rectangular stiffeners—one underlying the stem mold, the other the transom. These provide extra support at stem and stern, where the planking might have a tendency to pressure the molds out of position.

The spreader is used to hold the finished hull to the correct width amidships temporarily, while the rubrails are fitted and installed.

STRIP PLANKING

The prototype cradle dinghy was built of $1/4''$ strips ripped out of a $1/2''$-thick clear pine board. The resulting $1/4''$-thick by $1/2''$-wide strips were reasonably easy to work with, but $3/16''$-thick by $3/8''$-wide strips might have been easier to bend. A $12'' \times 16'$ board (or two $6'' \times 16'$ boards) will provide enough stock to plank the boat, with enough material left over to make the transom, floorboard, inner stem, and keel, if you choose to use pine for those pieces. (Cut these pieces out before you rip the remainder into strips. You must have a piece for ripping the strips that is at least 4' long.)

Rip the strips on a table saw fitted with a carbide-tooth or hollow-ground planer blade. (If you do not have a table saw, take your lumber to a custom-milling shop.) The goal is to produce a clean, smooth cut that is even in thickness; otherwise, the strips will not bend fairly. If you have access to a thickness planer, cut the strips $1/8''$ larger than the finished size—$5/16''$ thick by $1/2''$ wide—to allow for dressing them down on all four surfaces; the thickness planer will eliminate the sawblade swirls. Or you can sand the strips to final smoothness with a sanding block or a table sander.

TRANSOM

$1/2'' \times 9'' \times 15''$ pine, mahogany, or oak boards, or other hardwood of your choice, one piece.

(Note: If you cannot find acceptable stock as wide as 9", you can edge-glue two narrower boards. Do this on a flat surface, with waxed paper or plastic under the joint.)

FLOORBOARD

$1/2$" x 15" x 36". Use stock left over from the planking or transom, with supporting beams as described in Step 15.

If you have a piece of $1/4$" plywood, it is easier to use that, as supporting beams will not be required.

INNER AND OUTER STEMS

$1/2$" x 6" x 12" pine or hardwood (mahogany, cherry) of your choice, four pieces.

The inner and outer stems and the keel form the backbone of the boat. The planking is fastened to the inner stem as the boat is built; the outer stem is fastened on later as part of the finishing process.

KEEL

$1/2$" x 5" x 38" pine or hardwood (mahogany, cherry) of your choice, one piece.

RUBRAILS (GUNWALES)

$3/8$" x $1/2$" x 48" pine or hardwood (mahogany, cherry) of your choice, four pieces, solid or laminated.

KNEES AND BREASTHOOK

$1/2$" pine or hardwood of your choice, three pieces totaling about a board foot. These could be pieces left over from cutting out the keel or transom.

ROCKERS

1" x $8^1/2$" x 32" pine or hardwood (mahogany, cherry) of your choice, two pieces.

EPOXY AND FIBERGLASS

You will need approximately a gallon of epoxy resin along with the appropriate amount of hardener and $1^1/2$ yards of fine (2- or 4-ounce) fiberglass cloth.

FILLER AND VARNISH

FASTENINGS

$9/16$" steel staples, one box

4-penny or smaller common nails (small cabinet nails), $1/2$ lb.

$1/2$" No. 8 screws for temporary planking fastenings

$3/4$" No. 4 screws for rails, 2 doz.

$1^1/2$" No. 6 screws for knees and breasthook, 1 doz.

STEP-BY-STEP INSTRUCTIONS

STEP 1—ENLARGE THE PLANS

The reduced plans must be redrawn, enlarged by photocopying to full size, or purchased at full scale (see page 75). Using the set of full-sized plans eliminates redrawing or enlarging.

These reduced plans (see pages 80–83) are shown at 17% of the actual size. The easiest way to deal with the enlargement of the plans to full size is to have them enlarged by a professional reprographics firm. The photocopies obtained are not expensive, and are usually reliable. If you have access to an enlarging office-type photocopier, you can piece together the sheets and save some money, but it is complicated, time-consuming, and very imprecise. To do this, you'd make 600% copies on 11 x 17" sheets, and tape the copies together as necessary. Whichever process you use, trace the full-sized drawings onto the wood, or onto heavy building paper, using carbon paper beneath the drawing, and running over the lines with a pencil to transfer the carbon line. An ordinary sheet of carbon paper will do fine; just keep moving it along as you trace each section. With scissors, cut out the patterns and label them.

STEP 2—CONSTRUCT THE BOX BEAM

Build the box beam from $1/2''$ plywood (or particleboard)

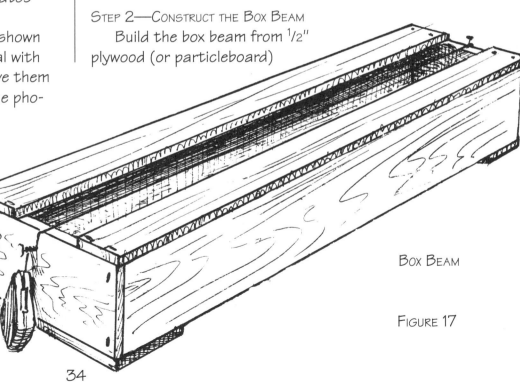

BOX BEAM

FIGURE 17

34

according to the dimensions given on the plans, making sure that all pieces are square to each other. Use sheetrock screws to fasten the pieces together.

Run a chalkline down the longitudinal center of the top of the box beam and tie it to nails driven into the centers of the ends, as shown in Figure 17. This chalkline will be used to center the molds on the box beam.

Referring to the plans, mark the position of each mold on top of the box beam with a line perpendicular to the center, and label it.

Check everything carefully, as a mistake here will throw off the fairness of the hull.

STEP 3—MAKE AND SET UP THE MOLDS

If you are using the gridwork method, you'll be tracing around each template. Otherwise, lay the mold plan on the 1/2" plywood, with carbon paper sandwiched in between, and trace each station mold pattern—first one side, then the other—directly onto the wood. Mark the centerline extending above and at the bottom of the mold plan.

The bottom edge of the plan should be perpendicular to the centerline; use it as a baseline for all the molds. This baseline will be where the mold sits on the box beam at its proper elevation.

Note that the sheerline, which represents the top edge of the planking when the hull is sitting right-side up, falls at a different point on each mold. For every mold, mark the sheerline on each side, and be sure the mold edge line extends from the sheerline down to the baseline.

The inner stem pattern is cut out of the same piece as the stem mold. Trace the inner edge from the plans; then, using a jigsaw, cut the inner stem pattern away from the stem mold. Then cut a few holes in the stem mold (shown in Figure 18) just large enough to allow for clamping the inner stem to the stem mold, later in Step 4. A hole saw in a drill is a good tool for this, if you have one; otherwise, use a jigsaw (or you could instead use temporary fastenings to hold the inner stem in place).

Carefully cut out the rest of the molds with a bandsaw or sabersaw, and check the edges for fairness. Smooth off any roughness with a file or sanding block. Complete marking a vertical centerline on both sides of each mold. Note that mold #1 has a small notch cut

out to accommodate the inner stem.

If you will be using the molds for more than one hull, or if there is any chance they will warp or twist in the building process (i.e., if you are working in a climate that has drastic fluctuations in humidity), or if you will take a long time (several weeks) to complete the planking, varnish the molds on all surfaces.

From ¹/₂" plywood cut out the two transom spacers and five 2"-wide cleats—one for each mold except the ones closest to the stem and transom (molds #1 and #7). For those, you will need to make rectangular stiffeners for the stem and for the transom to the dimensions indicated on the plans. Using sheetrock screws, fasten the stem mold to mold #1 along its centerline perpendicularly, and then fasten these to the stem stiffener. Fasten the transom spacers to mold #7, also with sheetrock screws, and fasten this unit to the transom stiffener. The spacers are designed to hold the transom mold at an angle. Fasten it to them at the proper location. Finally, fasten the rest of the molds to their cleats, as indicated on the plans.

Set up the molds on the box beam as indicated on the plans and shown in Figure 18, and fasten them in place with sheetrock screws. Drive the screws down through the cleats or stiffeners into the box beam. Eyeball the jig carefully from end to end. Be sure the centerline of each mold is aligned with the box-beam centerline, and that each mold is square to the centerline and plumb to the top of the box beam. Check all positions with a framing square. *This is very important, as the correct positioning of the molds ensures the proper shape of the hull—especially for such a small boat, where there would be a greater impact of error.*

Using a framing square, check the entire setup carefully to be certain that the center of each mold is aligned with the box-beam centerline, and is square to the centerline and plumb to the top of the box beam. You may need to shim certain molds with thin pieces of wood to correct any irregularities in cutting or alignment. Then run a spare planking strip or two—temporary battens—around the molds on top and on both sides of the setup, and tack them to the edges of the molds with finish nails. These will keep the molds from shifting during the planking process. Remove them as you plank up the hull.

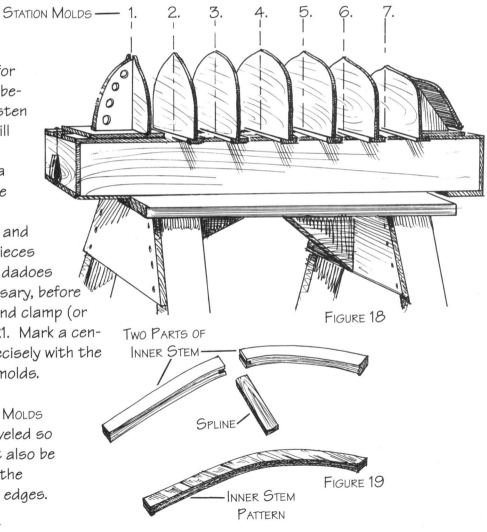

STATION MOLDS —— 1.   2.   3.   4.   5.   6.   7.

STEP 4—MAKE AND SET UP THE TRANSOM AND INNER STEM

Lay the transom pattern on the board you have selected for the transom, and trace around it. Cut out the transom and, being careful that it is aligned properly, clamp or temporarily fasten it to the transom mold, as shown in Figures 21 and 23; this will prevent it from being lifted by the strips during planking.

The inner stem is made in two parts joined together with a spline set in glue (see Figure 19). To lay out the parts, use the inner stem pattern or template (which you earlier cut out of the 1/2" plywood stem mold). Cut each half of the spline joint, and the spline itself, on a tablesaw, using extreme care as small pieces are difficult to handle with a tablesaw. Alternatively, cut the dadoes for the spline by hand. Dry-fit the pieces, reshaping as necessary, before gluing. Sand all four surfaces of the completed inner stem, and clamp (or temporarily fasten) it to the stem mold, as shown in Figure 21. Mark a centerline down its forward face, and check that it is lined up precisely with the centerline of the box beam and the vertical centerline of the molds.

FIGURE 18

TWO PARTS OF
INNER STEM

SPLINE

STEP 5—BEVEL THE EDGES OF THE INNER STEM, THE TRANSOM, AND THE MOLDS

The edges of the inner stem and the transom must be beveled so the planking strips will lie flat against them. The molds must also be beveled so as not to dent the strips in planking. Because of the shape of the hull, these bevels are not the same all along the edges.

FIGURE 19

INNER STEM
PATTERN

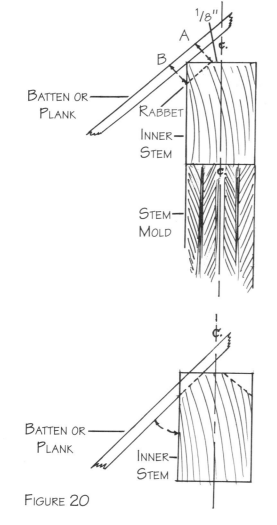

FIGURE 20

First, mark off the finished width of the forward face of the inner stem. Do this by drawing parallel lines 1/8" out from both sides of the stem face centerline. The width of the stem face will then be 1/4".

To bevel the stem, first mark the bevel as shown in Figure 20: Holding a batten or strip plank against mold #1 and the stem, measure the distance from the outside of the batten to the nearer line on the stem face (A). Now, with a pencil, mark the side of the stem where you measure the same distance between it and the outside edge of the batten (B). Connecting these two points will give you the planking angle (or rabbet of stem) at the top of the stem.

Run the batten along the stem at interval locations to scribe the changing bevel along the length of the stem. Use a sharp block plane to fair this bevel. Repeat this procedure for the bevel on the other side of the stem, and for the planking bevels on the transom and the molds.

STEP 6—CHECK THE SHEERLINE FOR FAIRNESS AND PREPARE THE MOLDS FOR PLANKING

Run the edge of a batten along the marks on the molds that delineate the sheerline, and tack the batten temporarily in place. Sight along the batten to check the sheerline for fairness. If it is not fair, adjust the batten where required until it is. You are trying to adjust a sweeping curve that is pleasing to the eye. This is important, as the sheerline is one of the most obvious elements of the finished boat. A hump in the sheer will stand out like a silo in a cornfield.

To prevent the planked hull from becoming glued to the building jig, apply duct tape to the edges of the molds and stem. The strips will stick somewhat to the duct tape, but the hull can still be removed from the molds. (You want the strips to stick a little to keep the planking from pulling away from the molds as you work.)

STEP 7—PLANK THE HULL

The hull is planked starting at the sheer, progressing toward the keel. Plank in pairs, laying a strip on one side of the hull and its mate on the other side. Be certain that each strip in a pair is identical in width to its mate; this is especially important later on, when some of the strips are tapered. If they are not identical, the strips will become staggered on either side of the hull and the aesthetics of the finished boat will be impaired, especially up in the bow where the run of the strips on each side of the boat meets.

If you can find some 4' scrap pieces of mahogany, red cedar, cherry, or another contrasting wood that is not too brittle, you might use strips of these to accent the sheerline. In the prototype cradle dinghy, a strip of mahogany was used for the third strip on each side (Figure 21).

Except for the first pair of strips, which are glued only at the ends, each strip will be edge-glued to the previ-

ous strip with epoxy, and held in place with staples driven into the molds. You may also need to use clamps, nails, and screws to hold the planks down at the stem and in places where the hull curves the most.

Because all staples used to hold the strips against the molds must be removed later, do not drive them all the way in. You will then have something to grip with your staple remover. Also, you don't want to leave unsightly divets in the wood, or have to sand them out. The best way to keep the top of the staples away from the wood is to apply several strips of masking or duct

FIGURE 21

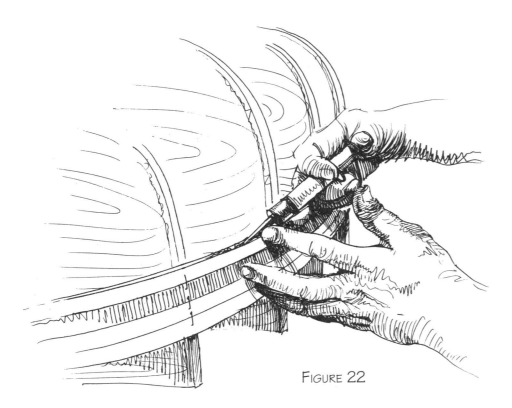

FIGURE 22

tape to the sole of your staple gun, building up a layer about $\frac{1}{16}''$ thick. The staple gun will automatically be held that distance away from the wood, and the tops of the staples will stand proud.

Epoxy begins to thicken slightly after about 10 minutes, so mix only enough glue at a time to hang a pair of strips. The best way to apply the glue is with a small syringe (Figure 22), available from hardware stores or epoxy companies; your next best choice is a small bristle brush.

Apply enough thickened epoxy so that, when the strip is clamped in place, epoxy squeezes out along the entire length of the joint—telling you that you do not have an epoxy-starved joint. Wipe the excess epoxy off the hull, inside and out, before it cures. The more gobs and drips of glue you leave behind, the more you have to sand off the hull later. Avoid getting epoxy on your skin. Wear rubber gloves, and wear safety glasses to protect your eyes. Read and heed the manufacturer's cautionary notes on the containers.

Glue the first strip only at the stem and transom, and fasten it against the molds with staples, making sure the strip follows the sheerline (marked on the molds) in a fair curve. Trim the strip flush with the transom and the inner stem. Then lay up its mate on the other side. Apply thickened epoxy to the edge of that strip, and at the transom and the stem, and bend on another strip. Fasten it in place with staples driven across the seam into the molds—i.e., one leg of a staple into the preceding strip, the other leg into the new strip. You'll follow the same procedure when hanging the rest of the strips.

It's important to take special care with these first few strips. Eyeball them carefully to be sure the sheer strips are aligned with each other. It's a good idea to let the first three strips set up overnight (or use screws at the stem and tran-

som). Then, trim the ends of the two planks that you edge-glued together. Continue this sequence, hanging the strips in pairs, one on each side—then trimming them, two at a time on alternating sides. It is best to trim as you go along; if you try to cut three or more strips at once, the saw will tend to bind up.

FIGURE 23

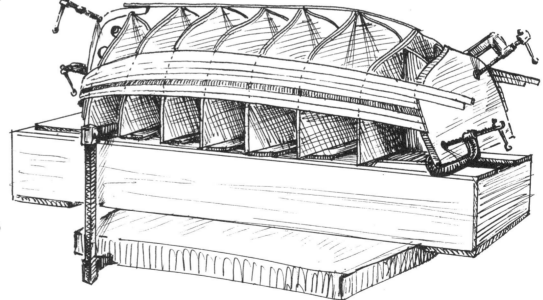

As you fit strips, you may need to bevel the edges so the strips will lie tightly against each other along their length. Try each strip, eyeball the bevel, then cut the bevel with a block plane set at a very fine depth. Take care not to bevel too much and create a gap on the inside. In many instances, especially when there is considerable twist in a strip, there will be slight gaps at the seams no matter how carefully you bevel. The gap-filling nature of thickened epoxy will take care of that problem. You can also use a clamp and wedge to close a gap. Fasten a medium-sized clamp across a gap to strips already set up (so they won't pull away), then tap a wedge of wood between the clamp and the latest strip, until the gap disappears (see Figure 24). Be careful not to snap the strip. If this happens, use a new strip and tap the wedge more gently.

Before you get to the extreme curves in the hull, take a spare strip and bend it until it snaps; this will give you an idea of how much pressure a strip can stand. At times quite a bit of twisting will be required to get the strips to lie flat against the molds. At the points of greatest twist, staples might not provide enough holding power. Try using very thin brads, or small nails; driving them in partway, at an angle, will help them resist the plank's tendency to pull away from the mold. Sometimes even this will not work, and you will have to drive a nail right down to the head. In the most extreme cases, you might have to use tiny screws to pull the strips down. Remember, however, that all fastenings are temporary; they must be removed later before you take the hull off the building jig. And, of course, the bigger the fastening, the bigger the hole it will make in the planking, and the more obvious the filled hole will be in the finished boat.

All along the stem, you'll need to use nails or screws

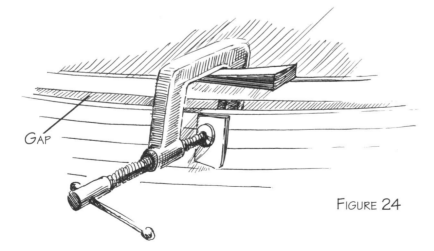

GAP

FIGURE 24

to hold the planks in place while gluing. The planks exert considerable pressure here; as you anchor them down, make sure you don't push so hard that the stem is moved off the centerline.

Because of the curve of the sheer, the first few strips will be a little stiff to bend on, as they will not only have to be bent around the bulge of the hull but also must be pushed down (remember, this boat is being built upside down) at their ends to follow the line of the sheer. However, the geometry of the boat is such that, as you plank toward the turn of the bilge (the area near the waterline), the downward curve at the ends of the strips will gradually decrease and the stiffness will decrease with it. Eventually there will be no downward curve and no stiffness. Shortly afterward, as you continue to hang strips, the geometry of the hull will cause the ends of the strips to curve upward, and the stiffness will gradually return. The farther you go, the greater the upward curve at the ends.

Somewhere around the turn of the bilge (Figure 25), if nothing were done in advance to prevent it, this upward curve at the ends of the strips would become so excessive that the strips would have to be twisted in the ex-

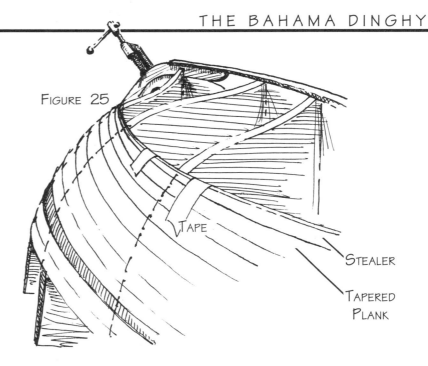

FIGURE 25

TAPE

STEALER

TAPERED PLANK

treme to get them to lie flat. Eventually the twist would become so great that the strips would break, or the temporary fastenings would not be able to hold the strips against the molds.

The wise strip-planker anticipates this eventuality and tapers the ends of a few strips to reduce the upward curve. In boatbuilding parlance, this is called "lining and spiling." To tell when it is time to do this, pay attention to the amount of twist required to make the strips

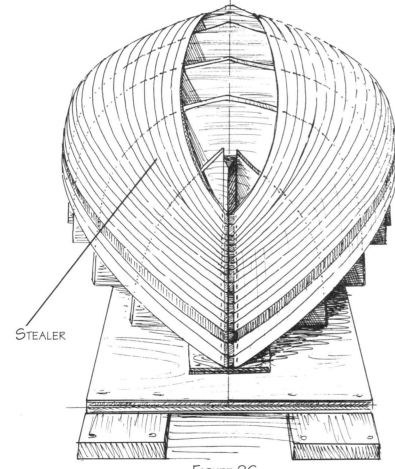

STEALER

FIGURE 26

lie flat. When this twist begins to increase, start to taper the strips. Also, watch the upward curve of the strips at their ends. If the curve starts to increase markedly from one strip to the next, it is time to taper a few strips.

The key element here is to anticipate change, not re-act after the change has taken place. In the prototype cradle boat to this design, built with $1/2''$ strips, the first tapered pair came at the tenth run of strips, then four full-length strips were tapered at their ends, then a stealer was put in, then a couple of full-length tapered strips were hung, then planking continued with full-width strips. (If $3/8''$-wide strips were used, the first tapering would have been required a few pairs later.) You can see this planking sequence clearly in Figure 26.

A stealer, sometimes called a "cheater," is a short, tapered strip centered in the middle of the run of plank-ing; its ends do not reach the stem or the transom. Stealers are required when tapering alone is not enough to remove excessive curvature at the ends of strips. Because a stealer does not reach the stem or the tran-som, holding its ends in place while the glue sets is sometimes difficult. One way to deal with this is to hold

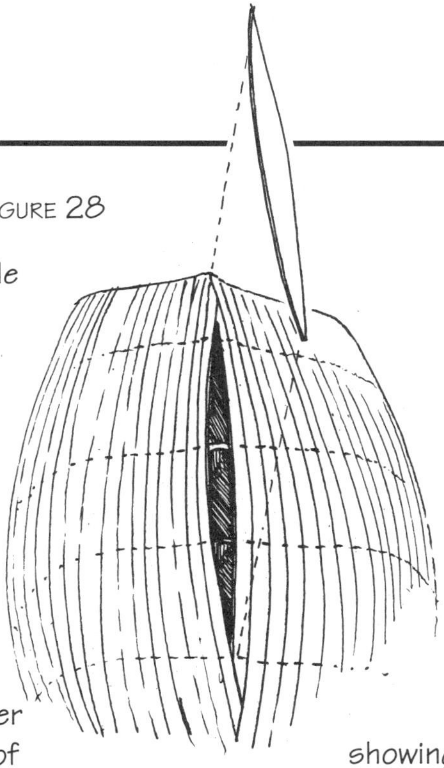

FIGURE 28

the ends with masking tape run from the outside of the planking, over the top of the stealer, and down the inside of the planking (see Figure 25). If that won't work, you can use very fine staples driven with an office stapler down through the edge of the stealer into the preceding strip. Keep in mind, however, that future sanding might expose such staples, so drive them carefully.

Taper the full-length strips and stealers in pairs, so they will be the same shape on both sides of the hull. Use a batten to draw the taper on the strips, being sure to curve only one side of each strip, leaving the other side straight. As shown in Figure 27, the curve should be cut on the side of the strip that will lie against the preceding strip, the one hung before this one. Tapers should be cut with a sharp block plane; eyeball them for fairness before installing the strip.

The dark side of using tapered strips and stealers is that they tend to show their edges after they are fastened in place, because they will twist differently. This, of course, affects the fairness of the hull. The more edges

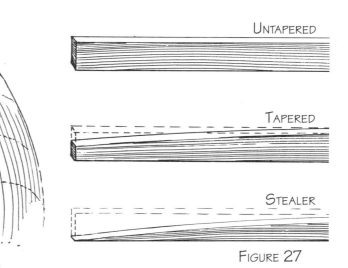

UNTAPERED

TAPERED

STEALER

FIGURE 27

showing, the more sanding and fairing required later.

As you approach the keel, the unplanked section will no longer run the length of the hull—the strips will be progressively shorter—so the ends of the strips must be tapered so they will lie along the centerline of the keel. Try your strips in place temporarily, mark and cut the taper, then bond and fasten the strips. When you get to the next-to-the-last strip, cut enough of a bevel on the edge facing the keel so that the last strip (Figure 28) can be pushed or wedged down into place.

Step 8—Pull the Temporary Fastenings

A day after the planking is completed and all epoxy has set, pull out *all* of the temporary staples, nails, and screws you have used. Avoid damaging the wood as you do this.

Dip a small brush in hot water and dab it around the holes made by the fastenings. The moisture will swell the wood slightly and close the holes somewhat, or at least it will make them smaller and less noticeable. Wood must be *thoroughly* dry before the next step—otherwise, the epoxy will not bond properly.

Use thickened epoxy, about the consistency of peanut butter, applied with a small auto-body squeegee to fill any holes and imperfections.

Step 9—Fair the Hull

Fair the hull with a hand-sanding block, starting with a coarse grit and following with medium and fine. (Or, use an electric disc sander *very carefully,* if you have one.) It is important to start with a coarse grit (60-grit is good), which will take down both hard and soft areas. Finish with a fine grit (220) to eliminate any sanding swirls. A finer grit at the start will take off more soft areas than hard and will therefore produce unfairness. If the boat is to be varnished, finish with 150- or 220-grit. You need not be quite as fussy if the hull is to be painted.

Avoid taking down too much of the planking, since it is very thin to begin with.

Sight along the hull as you go to be certain you are not "dishing" the hull in places, or creating flat spots. The finished surface should be an even, flowing curve.

Step 10—Fiberglass the Outside of the Hull

The outside of the hull should be covered with a single layer of fine fiberglass cloth (4-ounce or 2-ounce) set in epoxy.

With a roller, apply a coat of epoxy to saturate the surface of the wood, tipping off the surface with a foam-roller-cover "brush" (see description on page 3). Allow it to set up overnight. Wash the surface with water and paper towels and dry it thoroughly, then sand lightly.

Cut the cloth carefully to shape. As shown in Figure 29, it should cover just the strip-planked part of the hull, but not the transom. There is no need to cut the cloth on the bias; simply drape it over the hull and staple it lightly in areas where it tends to fall away from the surface. Let the cloth extend down past the edge or sheer of the hull. This will give you some excess cloth in case it gets pulled while you are fiberglassing.

Pour a small puddle of epoxy in the center of the hull and work it into the surrounding area with a plastic squeegee. Use care not to squeegee too vigorously, or you'll work air bubbles into the epoxy. Repeat the process, working out toward the edges. For this first coat, the cloth should have a dull, matte appearance, with no standing "puddles" remaining on the cloth's surface. You'll still be able to see the weave of the cloth—but that's all right, since you'll be filling the weave with subsequent coats.

After allowing the cloth to set up for several hours, begin applying additional coats of epoxy with a high-density foam roller. After rolling on a small section, tip it off with a roller-cover brush. You can then apply additional coats just as soon as the previous coat has cured enough to support the next coat's

weight. The object is to fill the weave.

After the last coat has been allowed to cure for several hours, and while the excess edges of the cloth are still somewhat flexible, trim the excess cloth with a sharp utility knife or with scissors.

After the epoxy has cured for a day or two, it is time to remove the hull from the building jig. All fastenings were removed before, so take a hammer and tap the

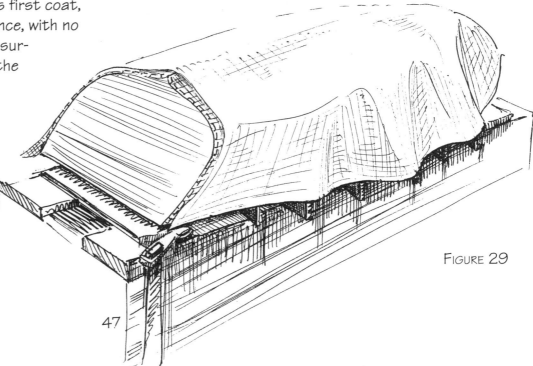

FIGURE 29

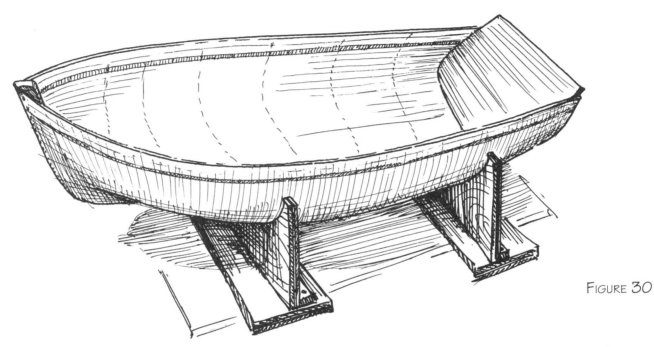

FIGURE 30

molds inside. This will unstick the hull from the tape on the molds.

Often the inner stem and transom are stuck to the molds. Tap some more to loosen the hull and pry the sides away from the molds. If only the stem is stuck, lift the hull gently off at the transom end.

The next step is to sand the inside of the hull and apply two coats of epoxy, as with the exterior. Set the hull in some supports, as shown in Figure 30, to keep it from rocking. Then sand the inside as you did the outside. Be careful if you are using an electric disc sander; it's very easy to dig into the wood with the edge of the sanding pad.

As with the outside, watch out for sanding swirl marks. When you think the hull is all sanded, check it over by wiping it with a cloth wet with alcohol. Any swirls

48

that really show should be sanded out and allowed to dry thoroughly before putting epoxy on. Fill any holes or imperfections with thickened epoxy.

There is no need to fiberglass the inside of the hull. Simply give it a couple of coats of epoxy, tipping the coating off with your roller-cover brush.

After letting the epoxy dry for a day or two, go over the hull, inside and out, with a final sanding until it is fair and smooth. Finish with a fine (150 or 220)-grit paper.

Step 11—Fit the Outer Stem and the Keel

The outer stem is joined to the keel in the same way as the two parts of the inner stem were joined, with a spline, at the hard curve or waterline (see Figure 32). As with the inner stem, you'll need to cut the spline joint and dry-fit the pieces before gluing and screwing the outer stem and keel to the hull.

So that the outer stem will fit flush against the inner stem, fair off the ends of the planking with a sander (a

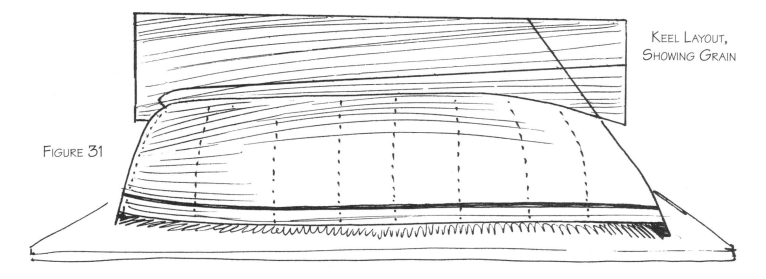

Keel Layout, Showing Grain

Figure 31

FIGURE 32

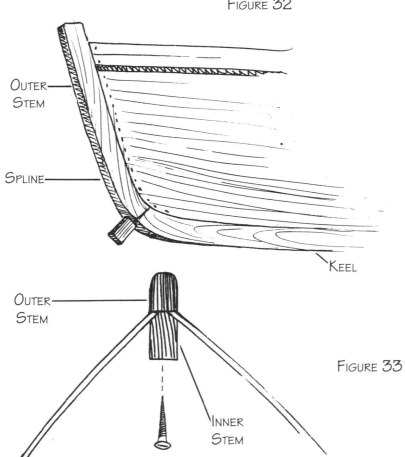

OUTER STEM

SPLINE

KEEL

OUTER STEM

INNER STEM

FIGURE 33

plane won't cut smoothly across the end-grain of the strips) perpendicular to the centerline. Set the outer stem in place with thickened epoxy to take care of any gaps, and, since it will be tapered to a finer edge later, fasten it with screws driven from the inside of the boat, through the inner stem into the outer stem (see Figure 33).

Cut out the keel according to the keel pattern. As shown in Figure 31, the wood grain should run roughly parallel with the bottom of the keel (to prevent splitting). Try it in place and trim to fit as necessary. Set the keel in thickened epoxy and fasten with screws driven from the inside of the boat, through the hull, and into the keel. Now, bond the spline joint of the stem and keel together. Clamp a temporary cleat to the transom parallel to the centerline; clamping the keel to the cleat (as in Figure 34) will keep it aligned and plumb.

STEP 12—FIT THE RUBRAILS (GUNWALES)

Because the strip-planked hull, with no frames, still "gives," you'll want to fit a temporary spreader athwart-ships to hold the sides apart while you fit and fasten the inner and outer rails. Cut the spreader with notched ends, to a width that will spread the hull the same distance as the 'midship mold, minus the thickness of the two inwales (see Figure 36). Set it in place amidships.

Now you're ready to put on the inner and outer rub-rails, or gunwales (see Figure 35). A nice-looking rail is about $\frac{1}{2}$" square. However, bending a solid piece on such a sharply curved hull will probably be too stressful. You may want to use a thinner piece, depending on the stiffness of the wood you have, or make laminated rails.

The choice of wood species for the gunwales is important. It's nice to have the rails match the transom, knees, and breasthook. But a hardwood such as oak or ash will bend more easily

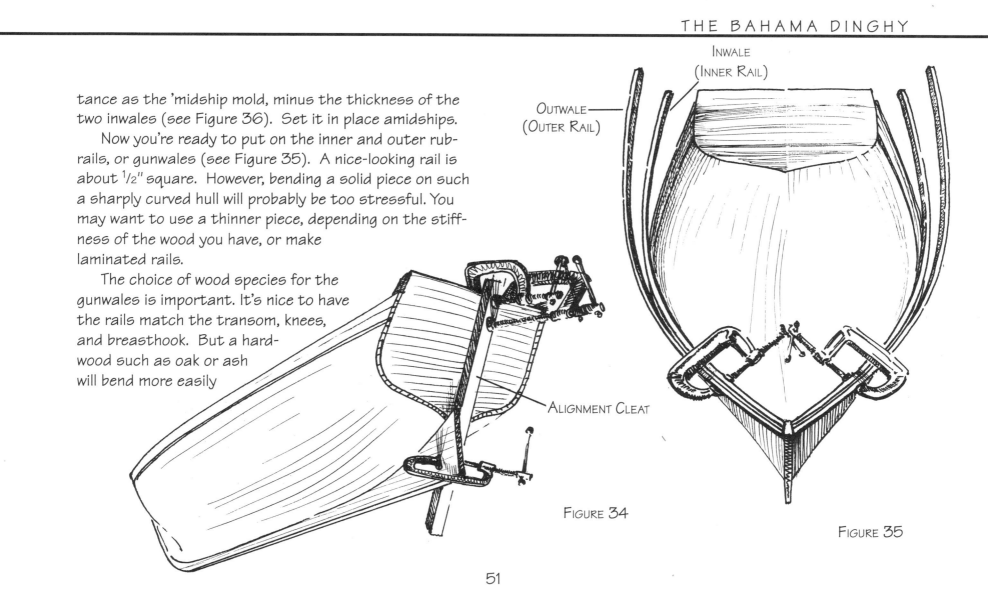

ALIGNMENT CLEAT

FIGURE 34

OUTWALE (OUTER RAIL)

INWALE (INNER RAIL)

FIGURE 35

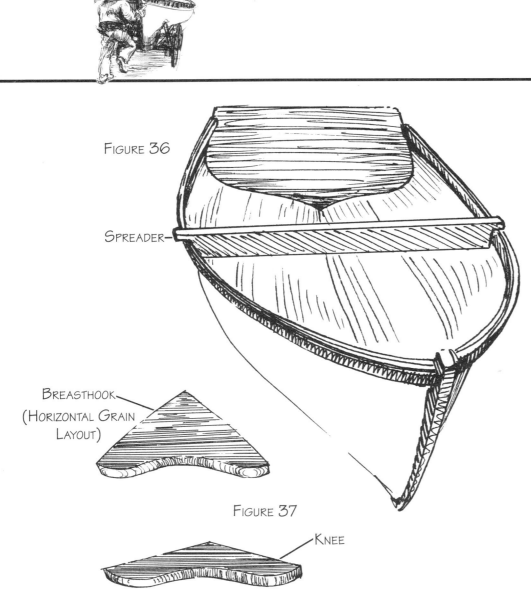

FIGURE 36

SPREADER—

BREASTHOOK
(HORIZONTAL GRAIN
LAYOUT)

FIGURE 37

KNEE

without snapping, especially if it's not kiln dried.

For the cradle shown in the illustrations, each rail was made of two pieces, laminated together, using the hull itself as a jig. (The rails were clamped to the hull, with waxed paper in between.) The rails were further shaped after they were cured.

To shape them, simply cut them on a table saw, if you have one, or sand them. You can also use a router with a small "bead and cove" bit ($1/8"$ or so). Taper the inwales at both ends a bit. This will make them easier to fit in, and you won't need so long a screw for fastening.

When you're ready to fasten on the rails, cut the forward ends to fit. You'll need to fit each outwale into the corner formed by the outer stem and the hull. Then, on each side, clamp both the inwale and the outwale in place against the hull, starting at the bow. Keep the spreader in place while you can, to maintain the proper hull width as you clamp on the rails. As you move toward the stern, trim the inwale end so that it will fit snugly inside the transom.

Drill and fasten the rails from the inside out, except at the bow and stern. This reduces the possibility of snapping them, compared to fastening from the outside.

At the bow and stern, you'll fasten from the outside through the gunwales and hull and into the breasthook and knees.

Step 13—Fit the Breasthook and Transom Knees

Lay out the patterns for the breasthook and transom knees on your wood so the grain follows the "hypotenuse" of each triangular shape, or the edge that will face inboard when installed (see Figure 37). This will give these pieces maximum strength to resist splitting; it will also ensure that the fastenings will not be driven straight into the end-grain, which would give a poor hold. Cut out the pieces, then bevel them to fit in place. Do this with a carpenter's bevel for a rough fit, then try them in place and fine-tune with a sharp block plane and a sanding block.

Fasten the breasthook and knees in place with glue and screws driven from the outside of the hull, through the rails. Eyeball the work carefully so the screws go straight into the knees and breasthook.

Step 14—Make the Rockers

Cut out the rockers according to the pattern. Mark their location as shown on the plans, try them in place, and with a spokeshave trim to fit as necessary, according to the shape of the hull (see Figure 38). Fasten with screws driven from the inside of the boat, through the hull, and into the rockers.

Figure 38 shows a small "sculling" notch that was cut, just for looks, in the transom of the prototype boat, using a jigsaw.

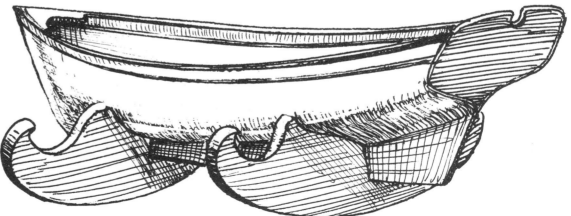

Figure 38

STEP 15—MAKE THE FLOORBOARD

If you are making the floorboard of ¼″ plywood, which is easiest, simply cut it out according to the pattern. Try it in place and trim around the edges as necessary so it will fit the sweep of the hull. Fasten it with two

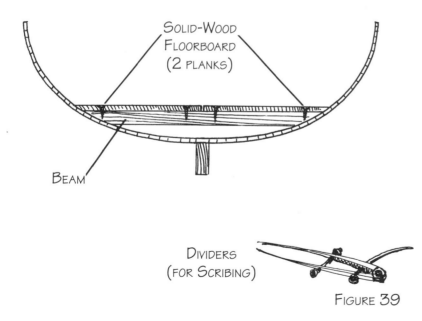

SOLID-WOOD FLOORBOARD (2 PLANKS)

BEAM

DIVIDERS (FOR SCRIBING)

FIGURE 39

screws at each side, driven down into the rockers.

If you are building the floorboard of solid, straight-grained wood, you'll need to support it with two beams (to keep it from buckling or splitting), each one located about over each rocker, running from one side of the hull to the other, as shown in Figure 39.

Cut the beams a minimum of ¾″ wide and the length of the floorboard where they will be installed. You'll need to use dividers to scribe the shape of the hull onto the end of each beam. Then cut along each scribed curve. Using sheetrock screws, fasten the beams to the hull from the outside in. Then put the floorboard in place and fasten it to the beams.

STEP 16—PAINT OR VARNISH

Seal all un-epoxied wood surfaces with a clear sealer if they are to be finished bright, or a pigmented sealer if they are to be painted. (Re-read the section "Filler, Paint, and Varnish" at the beginning of this chapter.) Sand lightly.

Varnish, paint, decorate, or embellish to your heart's content. (You may also wish to make a mattress as described on page 24.)

CHAPTER FOUR

A GALLERY OF CRADLE BOATS

Although the preceding pram and Bahama dinghy make fine little cradle boats, they by no means define the limits to the possibilities of what you can build. Ever since *WoodenBoat* magazine published the photograph of Guy Hammon's beautiful cradle pram (reproduced here), scores of cradle boats, from all over the world, have been brought to my attention. They range from the antique to the modern, from dories to runabouts, from elaborate ships-of-the-line to simple skiffs.

On the pages that follow you'll find photographs and brief descriptions of some of the most interesting of the lot, featured here to indicate the range of boat types suitable for cradle construction and to inspire those of you who are looking for the unique. Though some of these cradles were built by professionals, most were designed and built by amateurs, many of whom had never built a boat or a cradle before.

The common thread that runs through all of the cradle boats in this "gallery" is the thoughtfulness of their builders. Even the most simple boats—not much more than a few planks screwed and glued together and set on rockers—reflect an understanding of the preciousness of their infant crews. They also reflect an appreciation by the designers and builders of those elements that define the "boatiness" of a cradle boat. Few of them are seaworthy in the conventional sense of the word; after all, that is not the requirement of a cradle meant to rock a baby in the comfort of his or her home. But they look like boats, and they are stable enough to protect their crews.

These photographs might inspire you to design and build your own unique cradle boat, or even to modify one of the two designs presented previously—for example, by constructing davits for hanging, instead of rockers. To assist you, the following chapter lays out a few design principles for your consideration.

HANGING CRADLE
by Dick Cross of Eugene, Oregon

Dick Cross built this elegant boat in 1972 for his son. "Since my son's use," Dick says, "the cradle has had six long-term occupants and now hangs in the delivery room of a nearby birthing clinic. Its temporary crew members now number in the hundreds."

The cradle was built upside down over removable molds and took about 100 hours from start to finish. The transoms are ¼" walnut from a 90-year-old tree milled by Cross himself. The stempost and sternpost are rosewood, and the fastenings are copper nails.

"This cradle was slung about 3' off the floor," Dick says, "which not only kept it above floor drafts but also gave it a wonderful, slow swing of long duration. I always pushed the cradle with one finger against the sternpost, and there is still about a 6"-long spot that is polished smooth from rubbing."

CRADLE DORY by Paul Vigneux of Lakefield, Ontario

Built for little Veronica Best of Toronto, this flat-bottomed boat, reminiscent of a dory, has a removable mattress box. When Veronica grows up, she will be able to use the cradle as a toy box or a clothes box, a play pen, or even as a real boat in a small pond. The transom and bottom are pine, the planking is white cedar cut from Paul's farm, and the gunwales, outer stem, and rockers are cherry. "The only real drawback of this cradle," says Paul, "is that I used copper nails and roves for fastenings, and some of them had sharp and jagged edges. I should have used clench nails for the baby's safety."

LAPSTRAKE PULLING BOAT
by Paul Rollins of York, Maine

"I built this cradle for my daughter Ruth," says Paul, a professional boatbuilder. "I designed the boat myself, built it in about 100 hours during a fall lull in my business, and think of it as one of my more successful projects."

The keel is laminated mahogany, the sheer plank is black walnut, the rest of the planks are cedar, the frames are elm, the knees are natural oak crooks, and the rockers are black locust with a natural sweep to the grain. The mattress is a custom-made futon.

ROCKING DORY (below left)
by Charles Downs of Waxhaw, North Carolina

This handsome dory was built by Charles Downs to entertain his nephew, Cap'n Jamie Wilson. "The rockers," Charles says, "are of such a design that Jamie can play anywhere in the boat without capsizing it; he can even rock it while sitting in the bow or stern. The width between the rockers is about 14", which is important for stability. The seat rests on a solid block fastened to the bottom of the boat to prevent Jamie from hooking his legs under it and injuring himself."

DINGHY (below right)
by Lawrence Hendricks of New Preston, Connecticut

A commission to professional woodworker Lawrence Hendricks, this cold-molded dinghy was built using the Gougeon WEST System and 1/16" African mahogany veneers. "Lofting the construction form was the most difficult part," Larry says. "The rest of the construction was straightforward. As I worked, the thoughts that came to mind were of the launching of a new life, of the nursery rhyme 'Wynkin, Blynkin, and Nod,' and even of Moses in his basket on the Nile."

THE "BABY TENDER" (below)
by Warren Jordan of South Beach, Oregon

This lapstrake yacht tender, slung in traditional davits, was built by a professional boatbuilder and ex-commercial fisherman. The planking is Alaska yellow cedar over steam-bent white oak frames, copper riveted. The backbone, transom, and all interior joinery are of cherry. The davits are also cherry, and all of the principal parts are held together with brass pins, which allow easy disassembly. Plans are available for building this boat; see the listing for Jordan Wood Boats in the Appendix.

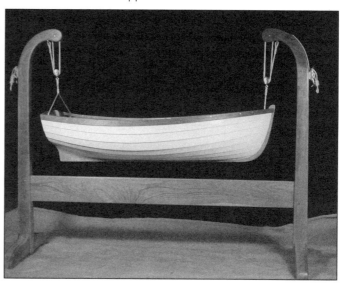

SANDBAGGER BABY BED (above)
by Jean-Yves Poirier of Aigrefeuille, France

More like a bed than a cradle, this elegant boat built by Poirier for his son Clement is based on a 19th-century American sandbagger. It was strip-planked with epoxy adhesive. The planking is yellow pine; the stem, keel, and rocker structure are Afromorsia, which is similar to teak. "As small as this boat is," Jean-Yves says, "my garage-boatyard was so small that the main part of the work was done outside on the sidewalk!"

SKIFF (above)
by Dan Brown of Beaufort, South Carolina, for his daughter Blythe. "She was quick to build—as was Blythe, who came a couple of months before we expected!"

PULLING BOAT (left)
by Dale Krause of Corpus Christi, Texas, for his son Casey. "I got the idea from an antique 4' double-ended cradle boat I saw in the Harbor Island lighthouse."

FLOATING SKIFF (below)
by Captain Robert Merrick, USN (ret.), of White-Stone, Virginia, for his grandson Logan. "The design is strictly eyeball, as the only given was my daughter's guesstimate that her baby would be about 40" long when old enough to use the cradle."

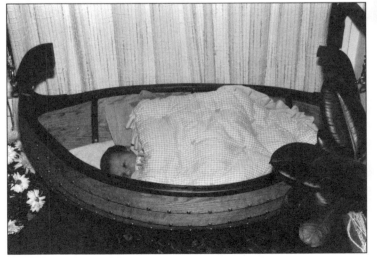

VIKING LONGBOAT (left)
by Jonathan Knight for his daughter Kathryn. "The davits ensure that any motion of the child will set up a gentle but safe motion to promote restful sleep for all of us."

ROCK-'N'-ROLLING DORY
by Buck Smith of Green's Island, Maine

Designed and built by our illustrious illustrator, this dory is more appropriate as a toy for an older child than as a cradle for a baby. That's Buck's son Bowen at the controls, taking his mother Becky for a cruise on the bounding sea. A smaller version of this design was eventually put into production as the now-famous Gloucester Rocker.

LAPSTRAKE
SKIFF
by Ben Stone
of Ithaca, New York

This hanging skiff, slung from the ceiling, is based on an 8' yacht tender designed by Iain Oughtred. Like many of Iain's designs, it features frameless construction and glued-lap plywood planking. Reduced to 41% of the full-sized skiff, it exhibits all of the elements of a successful cradle boat: considerable beam in relation to length, a wide bottom to hold the mattress, sufficient depth to prevent the baby from falling out, and no appurtenances to cause injury to the crew.

PRAM
by Dennis Cumin of Billings, Montana

This is an unusual arrangement, as the davits that support the cradle at both ends are in the shape of pelicans, whose bills are gripping the transoms. The cradle is strip-planked of cedar milled from a fence post, with oak, mahogany, and walnut joinery. "When Chad grows out of his cradle boat," says Dennis, "I'll remove it from the davits and fit it out with oars and wheels so he can 'barrow his toys around in it."

DOUBLE-ENDER
by Steve Sirch of South Burlington, Vermont

Steve built this lapstrake-plywood boat for his son Austin, who slept aboard daily for his first three months. "But he was a large baby," says Steve, "100th percentile at that time, and may have been better off in a boat with a transom of the same length or a bit longer. Near the end of his voyage he had a tendency to throw a leg overboard while sleeping. Austin's boat now sits in his room and holds his toys. Winnie-the-Pooh is the new master."

RUNABOUT
by Chris Smith of Holland, Michigan

Built by Chris Smith in 1951 for his daughter Susan, this little boat is planked in mahogany, just like the classic Chris-Craft runabouts of the era. "The boat crib is still in excellent condition," says Chris, "and it stands ready to cradle many more great-great-grand-children of my grandfather, Christopher C. Smith, founder of Chris-Craft."

ANTIQUE CRADLE-SHIP (*above*)
in the Museum of Faluas, Aranjuez, Spain

This ship-of-the-line, complete with gilded carvings, dates from the late 18th century. It belonged to King Fernando VII when he was a infant. According to Bill Durham, who photographed the cradle, "A first-rate cradle did not save Fernando from having a difficult reign—captured by Napoleon, lost the Americas, etc."

Stern-quarter detail of Fernando VII's ship-cradle.

ANTIQUE CRADLE DINGHY (*below*) in the Otago Museum, Dunedin, New Zealand

This little dinghy was built in 1888 by the ship's carpenter of the full-rigged sailing ship CLACK-MANSHIRE to the order of the skipper, Captain William Cauper, for his granddaughter Margaret. Stuart Reid, who has examined the cradle in detail, says, "The boat is clinker built in a very craftsman-like manner and weighs only about 14 pounds."

ANTIQUE CRADLE BOAT ON WHEELS
discovered in Harrisburg, Pennsylvania

The inventor of this cradle was Abner Woodward of Shelburne Falls, Massachusetts, who was issued a patent for its design. It was built by Ford Johnson & Company of Michigan City, Indiana. According to John Ensminger, the owner of the cradle, the patent documentation reads in part: "The object of my invention is to provide a cradle that is especially convenient and serviceable. It is light in weight and at the same time, on account of its peculiar construction, it is elastic in all its parts, susceptible to the slightest motion, and therefore easily swung."

ANTIQUE LAPSTRAKE LIFEBOAT
in Culzean Castle, Ayr, Scotland

The beauty of this boat lies both in the exquisite construction, complete with copper-riveted planks, and the care with which the hull was lined for the comfort of the baby. Robert Williams, who studied the cradle on site at the castle, says that the furnishings in the castle are from the early 19th century and, presumably, this cradle boat dates to that period.

CHAPTER FIVE

ADAPTING A DESIGN

One of the pleasures of cradle-boat building is that many small craft can be adapted for the purpose. Just as the cradle pram and Bahama dinghy described in the preceding chapters are modifications of full-scale boats, there are any number of boats whose plans can be modified to produce fine little rocking-and-rolling craft. Whether you find this easy or difficult to do depends on your boatbuilding and woodworking experience, and your understanding of the elements of hull design and stability. A miniature Whitehall, with carvel planking over steam-bent frames, would tax the abilities of all but the most able boatbuilders. A flatiron skiff with a cross-planked bottom, however, is well within the capabilities of anyone who can read boat plans and use simple hand tools. Figure 40 shows five possible adaptations of traditional hull types.

There isn't much difference between building a real boat and building a cradle boat. In some respects the cradle boat is easier, because the hull need not be made watertight and the ravages of wind and water need not be considered. So, if

you decide to go beyond the two designs and construction methods presented in this book and build your own customized cradle boat, there are plenty of books on wooden boat building to guide you along (see the Bibliography).

Several types of small craft are ideal for adaptation to cradle boats. Any boat that resembles in shape a conventional cradle will fit the bill. In general, these are boats with high freeboard, great width in relation to length, a wide bottom, and a U-shaped (rather than V-shaped) mid-section. Many times, the purpose of a boat will dictate its suitability. Yacht tenders, for example, are usually wide, and short, and are designed with carrying capacity in mind. Peapods, which were originally built for fishing and lobstering, are wide and most have a higher-than-normal freeboard for their length.

In general, boats that are designed for speed make poor cradle boats. They tend to be too narrow, low-sided, and sometimes unstable. Fast pulling boats, canoes, skimming-dish catboats, some dories, and the like fit in this category. To be sure, the undesirable elements in these boats can be

designed out of them—they can be widened, and the sides can be raised—but such changes can so alter their characteristics that they will start to look like another boat type. A redesigned canoe will look more like a peapod than a canoe (though authentic construction, if it is used, will reveal its origins). To some cradle builders, this will not matter much; but to others, it will be a sign of a lack of understanding of boat design.

When you get right down to it, a good cradle boat is a caricature of a real boat. It has all of the elements of a real boat, and then some. Exaggeration is the order of the day. The sheer is greater, the curves of the hull are more pronounced, the crown of the transom is higher, the stem stands at a cockier angle. A plain, ordinary flatiron skiff scaled down to cradle-boat size, without being spiced up aesthetically, makes a plain, ordinary, dull cradle boat. Put a little more curve in the sheer, though, and rake the transom farther aft a bit, and you have a cradle boat that will put a smile on anyone's face.

But you can't get so carried away with the aesthetics that you forget about the much more important safety aspects. A cradle boat, after all, is for a baby, and the baby's

health and safety are of the greatest importance. So here are a few vital principles for your consideration:

Keep in mind at all times the stability of the boat. The lower the center of gravity, the more stable the boat will be. High, narrow designs should be rejected. Even wide, low boats can have a problem if the floorboard or mattress is too high in the cradle. A design that is wide at the sheer but narrow at the bottom, for example, will necessitate mounting the floorboard rather high in the boat to provide room for the baby, thereby raising the center of gravity.

Make sure there is enough length and width for the baby. You don't want the poor little thing banging into the ends or the sides. Even if there is ample room, make provision for padding.

Consider carefully the design of the rockers. You can increase the stability of the cradle by increasing the width of the rockers and reducing the curve on the bottom of the rockers. Well-designed rockers can be made even safer by putting a little reverse curve at the tips (an example is shown in Figure 41). This way, if the cradle should rock too far—when, for example, the baby's little brother or sister leans on the rail to get a better look inside—the reverse

Keelboat

Peapod

Dory

Skiff

Viking Boat

Figure 40

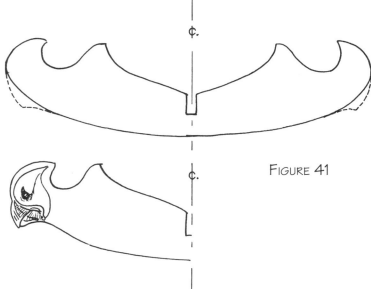

FIGURE 41

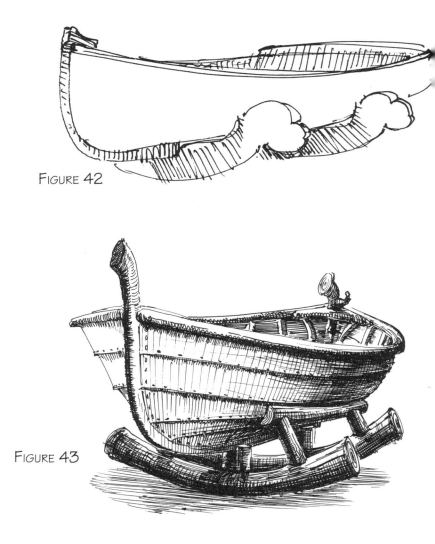

FIGURE 42

FIGURE 43

curve should prevent the cradle from tipping over. Figures 42 and 43 show two other rocker styles.

The construction of the boat is important. The ideal cradle boat has no frames for the baby to bang up against, or jam his or her fingers behind if the hull is lapstrake planked. If frames are necessary, try to position them so there won't be any near the baby's head.

And, of course, do not use any toxic materials in the finish of the boat.

BIBLIOGRAPHY

BOOKS ON BOATBUILDING

Though there are no books other than this one on cradle-boat building as such, there are a number of good books on the art and craft of building wooden boats. These books cover a variety of construction techniques and would be valuable to anyone who intends to adapt the design of a full-scale boat and build it as a cradle, or produce and build an original cradle-boat design.

Boatbuilding, by Howard I. Chapelle. 1941. W.W. Norton, 500 Fifth Ave., New York, NY 10036.

Traditional plank-on-frame construction; flat-, V-, and round-bottomed boats. Contains study plans for several designs.

Boatbuilding in Your Own Back Yard, by S.S. Rabl. 1958. Cornell Maritime Press, 306 East Water St., Centreville, MD 21617.

Plank-on-frame and plywood construction. Addresses the concerns of the amateur builder. Contains usable building plans.

Boatbuilding Manual, by Robert M. Steward. Third revised edition, 1987. International Marine Publishing Company, Camden, ME 04843.

Survey of all types of construction. Contains study plans.

How to Build a Wooden Boat, by David C. (Bud) McIntosh and Samuel F. Manning. 1987. WoodenBoat Publications, P.O. Box 78, Brooklin, ME 04616.

Beautifully written and thoroughly illustrated treatise on the construction of the traditional cruising boat.

Lapstrake Boatbuilding, Volumes 1 and 2, by Walter J. Simmons. 1980. Ducktrap Woodworking, Lincolnville, ME 04849.

Building such small craft as peapods, wherries, and light canoes.

Ultralight Boatbuilding, by Thomas J. Hill. 1987. International Marine Publishing Company, Camden, ME 04843.

Lapstrake plywood construction, using few or no frames. Study plans for several small boats.

Building Classic Small Craft, Volumes 1 and 2, by John Gardner. 1977. International Marine Publishing Company, Camden, ME 04843.

How to build specific boats, including dories, Whitehalls, peapods, dinghies, punts, etc. Both volumes include plans with offsets.

Boatbuilding with Plywood, by Glen L. Witt. 1978. Glen-L Marine Designs, 9152 Rosecrans, Bellflower, CA 90706.

The single most detailed explanation of plywood boatbuilding.

Instant Boats, by Harold H. Payson. 1979. H.H. Payson & Co., Pleasant Beach Rd., South Thomaston, ME 04858.

Simple plywood boatbuilding. Includes plans for several boats.

Build the New Instant Boats, by Harold H. Payson. 1984. International Marine Publishing Company, Camden, ME 04843.

Tack-and-tape plywood boatbuilding. Includes plans for several boats.

Go Build Your Own Boat!, by Harold H. Payson. 1987. H.H. Payson & Co., Pleasant Beach Rd., South Thomaston, ME 04858.

How to build small boats; includes details of plank-on-frame and plywood construction, plus valuable information on how to design your own boat by constructing a half model first.

How to Build the Catspaw Dinghy: A Boat for Oar and Sail, by the Editors of WoodenBoat. 1980. WoodenBoat Publications, P.O. Box 78, Brooklin, ME 04616.

A modified version of a Herreshoff dinghy; carvel construction. Contains study plans and step-by-step photographs.

Building the Nutshell Pram, by Maynard Bray. 1987. WoodenBoat Publications, P.O. Box 78, Brooklin, ME 04616.

Very adaptable to cradle-boat building; plywood construction. Contains study plans.

Canoecraft, by Ted Moores and Merilyn Mohr. 1983. Camden House Publishing, Ltd., Camden East, Ontario, Canada.

Though canoes are not particularly suitable designs for cradle boats, the value of this book is its excellent discussion of strip planking.

The Gougeon Brothers on Boat Construction, by the Gougeon Brothers. Revised edition, 1985. Gougeon Brothers, Bay City, MI 48707.

Technical manual on cold-molded construction, with additional material on strip planking and boatbuilding with plywood. First rate.

BOOKS ON PLANS
(see also the Appendix,
"Cradle Boat Plans")

The following books contain study plans only—not complete building plans. They are, in effect, plans catalogs from which building plans can be ordered.

Atkin Designs. 1987. P.O. Box 3005, Noroton, CT 06820.

Rowboats and dinghies designed by John and William Atkin. Lapstrake, plywood, and carvel construction.

Fifty Wooden Boats: A Catalog of Building Plans, Vol. I. 1984. WoodenBoat Publications, P.O. Box 78, Brooklin, ME 04616.

Prams, dinghies, skiffs, and tenders. Designs by Joel White, Charles Wittholz, Iain Oughtred, and others, for all methods of construction.

Thirty Wooden Boats: A Second Catalog of Building Plans. 1988. WoodenBoat Publications, P.O. Box 78, Brooklin, ME 04616.

Among others, includes Iain Oughtred-designed prams, dinghies, and canoes. Frameless, lapstrake plywood construction.

Glen-L Marine Designs: Book of Boat Designs. Glen-L Marine, 9152 Rosecrans, Bellflower, CA 90706.

Easy-to-build skiffs and prams. Designs for plywood construction by Glen L. Witt.

R.H. Baker Boats: A Catalog of Building Plans. Baker Boat Works, 29 Drift Rd., Westport, MA 02790.

Dinghies and skiffs, wherries, peapods, catboats. Traditional plank-on-frame construction. Designs by Robert (Bob) H. Baker.

APPENDIX

SOURCES OF SUPPLY COMPILED BY THE EDITORS OF WOODENBOAT MAGAZINE

CRADLE BOAT PLANS

Jordan Wood Boats
P.O. Box 194
South Beach, OR 97366
("Baby Tender," 45" x 22" lapstrake
dinghy with davits; full-sized patterns.)

RKL Boatworks
(Full-sized plans for building the
Bahama dinghy are available. See
page 75.)

WoodenBoat Publications
(Cradle pram, full-sized plans available.
See page 75.)

PLYWOOD WITH SPECIALTY
VENEERS

Boulter Plywood Corp.
24 Broadway
Somerville, MA 02145

Bre Lumber
10741 Carter Rd.
Traverse City, MI 49684
616-946-0043

Flounder Bay Lumber
3rd and O Streets
Anacortes, WA 98221

Harbor Sales Company
1401 Russell St.
Baltimore, MD 21230
1-800-345-1712

Hudson Marine
Plywoods
P.O. Box 1184
Elkhart, IN 46515
219-262-3666
—or—
P.O. Box 58
Ashley, PA 18706

JMB/McCausey
36329 Harper Ave.
Mt. Clemens, MI 48043
313-792-5210

Shell Lumber and
Hardware Co.
2733 S.W. 27th Ave.
Miami, FL 33133
305-856-6401

West Wind Hardwoods
10230 Bowerbank Rd.
Sydney, BC,
     Canada V8L 3S8
604-656-0848

LUMBER

Bre Lumber
(address under Plywood)

East Teak of WA
8510 212th St. S.E.
Woodinville, WA 98072
206-483-2550

Hartwood
P.O. Box 323
East Golden Lane
New Oxford, PA 17350
717-624-4323

Hudson Marine Plywoods
(address under Plywood)

Keiver-Willard Lumber Corp.
11-13 Graf Rd.
Newburyport, MA 01950

Niedermeyer USA
P.O. Box 6737
Portland, OR 97228
503-222-2208

North Atlantic Lumber
144 Fore St.
Portland, ME 04101
207-772-2450

Olyve Hardwoods
Wilmington, NC 28401
919-686-4611

Shell Lumber and Hardware Co.
(address under Plywood)

West Wind Hardwoods
(address under Plywood)

GLUES & RESINS

Chem-Tec, Inc.
4669 Lander Rd.
Chagrin Falls, OH 44022
212-248-0770

Detco Marine
P.O. Box 1246
Newport Beach, CA 92663
714-631-8480

Fibre Glass-Evercoat
6600 Cornell Rd.
Cincinnati, OH 45242
513-489-7600

Gougeon Bros.
WEST SYSTEM Epoxy
P.O. Box X908
Bay City, MI 48707
517-684-7286

Industrial Formulators of CanadLtd.
3824 William Street
Burnaby, BC, Canada V5C 3H9
604-294-6315

Lan-O-Sheen
1105 Homer St.
St. Paul, MN 55116
612-224-5681

Oceana Distributors, Ltd.
1811 Virginia St.
Annapolis, MD 21401
800-523-8890

Sika Corporation
Chemseco Division
4800 Blue Parkway
Kansas City, MO 64130
800-323-5926

Smith & Company
5100 Channel St.
Richmond, CA 94804
415–237–68 42

System Three Resins
P.O. Box 70436
Seattle, WA 98107
206–782–7076

FINISHES

Amazon Teak Oil
P.O. Box 530156
Miami Shores, FL 33153
800–832–5645

Classic Yacht Finishes
Philadelphia Resins Corp.
P.O. Box 454
Montgomeryville, PA 18936
215–855–8450

Deks Olje
The Flood Company
Hudson, OH 44236
216–650–4070

Epifanes U.S.A.
1218 S.W. First Ave.
Fort Lauderdale, FL 33315
305–467–8325

Oceana Distributors, Ltd.
(address under Glues & Resins)

Sterling
Detco Marine
(address under Glues & Resins)

Regatta, Baltic & Interlux
International Paint
2270 Morris Ave.
Union, NJ 07083
800–INTRLUX

U.S. Paint
831 South 21st St.
St. Louis, MO
63103–3092
314–621–0525

ValSpar Corp.
1191 South Wheeling Rd.
Wheeling, IL 60090
312–520–8583

Z-Spar
Kop-Coat, Inc.
Koppers Building
Pittsburgh, PA 15219
A.F.M. Enterprises*
1140 Stacey Ct.
Riverside, CA 92507
714–781–6860

AURO Plantchemistry*
Sinan Company
P.O. Box 857
Davis, CA 95617–0857
916–753–3104

LIVOS PlantChemistry*
1365 Rufina Circle
Santa Fe, NM 87501
505–438–3448
800–621–2591 (orders)

"Safe & Simple" finishes by Carver
    Tripp*
The Woodworker's Store
21801 Industrial Blvd.
Rogers, MN 55374
612–428–4101

TOOLS & FASTENINGS

Brookstone
127 Vose Farm Rd.
Peterborough, NH
03458

Delta International
Machinery Corp.
246 Alpha Drive
Pittsburgh, PA 15238
800–438–2486

Garrett Wade Co.
161 Avenue of the Americas
New York, NY 10013

Hamilton Marine
Main St.
Searsport, ME 04974
207–548–2985

Jamestown Distributors
28 Narragansett Ave.
Jamestown, RI 02835
1–800–423–0030

Standard Fastenings
800 Mt. Pleasant St.
New Bedford, MA 02741
—or—

991 S.W. 40th Ave.
Fort Lauderdale, FL 33317
1–800–678–8811

Tool Crib of the North
Div. of Acme Electric
P.O. Box 1716
Grand Forks, ND
58206–1716

Trendlines
375 Beachum St.
Chelsea, MA 02150

Wilke Machinery Co.
3230 Susquehanna
    Trail North
York, PA 17402
717–764–5000

Williams & Hussey
P.O. Box 1149
Wilton, NH 03086
603–654–6828

Woodcraft Supply Corp.
210 Wood County
    Industrial Park
P.O. Box 1686
Parkersburg, WV,
    26102–1686

The Wooden Boat Shop
1007 N.E. Boat St.
Seattle, WA 98105
800–933–3600
206–634–3600

* Specialize in non-toxic finishes

BUILDING PLANS AND PATTERNS

If the two cradle boats featured in this book appeal to you, and you'd like to build one or both of them, there are reduced plans and patterns with grids and dimensions on the following pages to help you do so. There are two ways of utilizing these reduced plans: having them photographically expanded, or redrawing the plans with expanded dimensions. If you choose the latter method, and are concerned about getting the curved shapes to match the original, you may want to lay out a grid of one inch squares on a sheet of 36" x 48" paper. The grid on the reduced plans is one-sixth of an inch because they must be expanded 600%. If you follow the dimensioned measurements, and use the grid system to develop the curved lines, you should have no trouble expanding the plans. If you prefer to have the plans expanded photographically, you will need to take the pages to a blueprint or reprographics source, and have the drawings you need blown up on an engineering enlargement photocopier. You should, however, be prepared to make some adjustments, since there is likely to be some distortion in this much enlargement. The rules and grids provide reference dimensions, and the sheets should be fairly close. Do not worry too much about exact matching if it continues to elude you, but do the best you can to make the dimensions match their measurements. In any case, if there is any question about the percentage, the reference rules should always be used as the standard.

For those who would prefer to work with supplied plans, they may be purchased separately. The full-sized *cradle pram* plans are available for $18 per set from: WoodenBoat Plans, P.O. Box 78, Brooklin, ME 04616, (207) 359–4647.

The full-sized *cradle dinghy* plans are available at $40 per set from: RKL Boatworks, Pretty Marsh Road, Mount Desert, ME 04660, (207) 244–5997.

Or, as we've suggested, you may want to develop your own plans for your own cradle boat. Whatever your choice, we wish you good luck and fair winds.

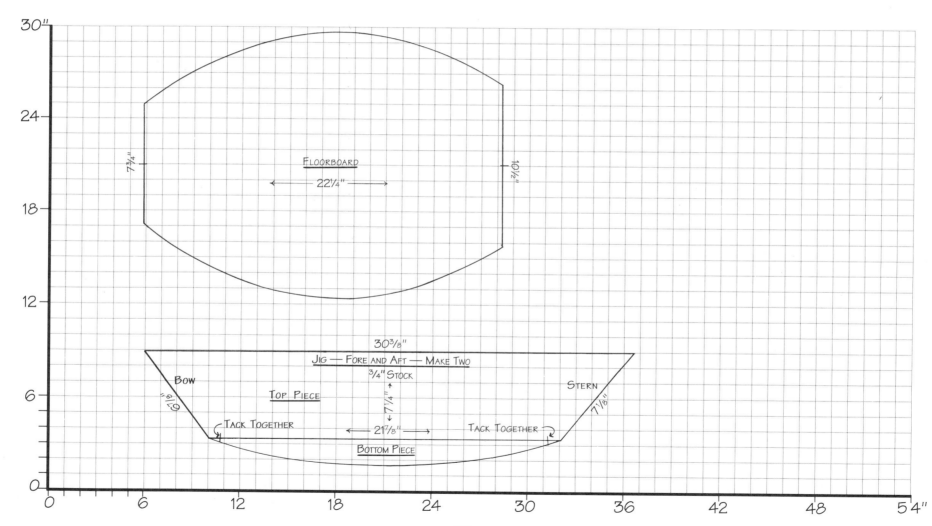

30"

24"

18"

12"

6"

0

7¾"

FLOORBOARD

← 22¼" →

10½"

30⅜"

JIG — FORE AND AFT — MAKE TWO

¾" STOCK

BOW

6⅛"

TOP PIECE

7¼"

STERN

7⅛"

TACK TOGETHER

← 21⅞" →

TACK TOGETHER

BOTTOM PIECE

0   6   12   18   24   30   36   42   48   54"

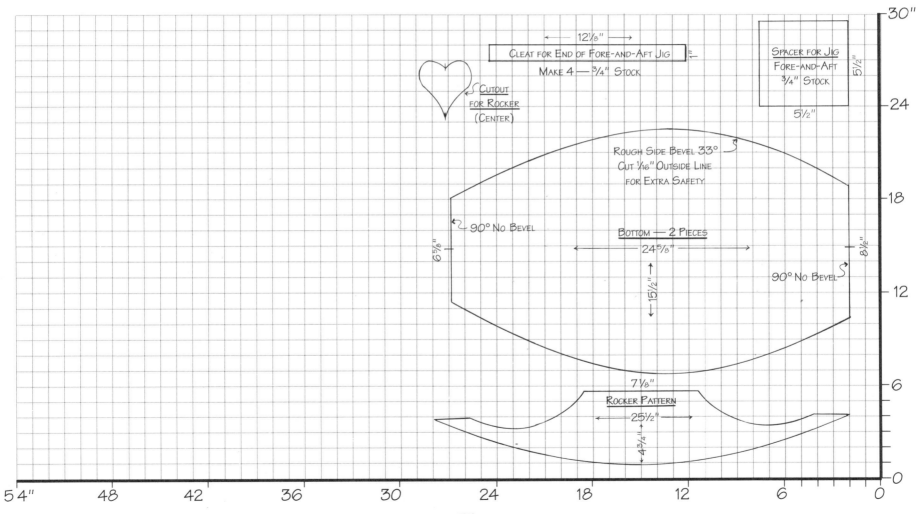

12⅛"

Cleat for End of Fore-and-Aft Jig

Make 4 — ¾" Stock

Spacer for Jig
Fore-and-Aft
¾" Stock

5½"

5½"

Cutout
for Rocker
(Center)

Rough Side Bevel 33°
Cut 1/16" Outside Line
for Extra Safety

90° No Bevel

Bottom — 2 Pieces

24⅝"

6⅝"

8½"

15½"

90° No Bevel

7⅛"

Rocker Pattern

25½"

4¾"

30"

24

18

12

6

0

54"   48   42   36   30   24   18   12   6   0

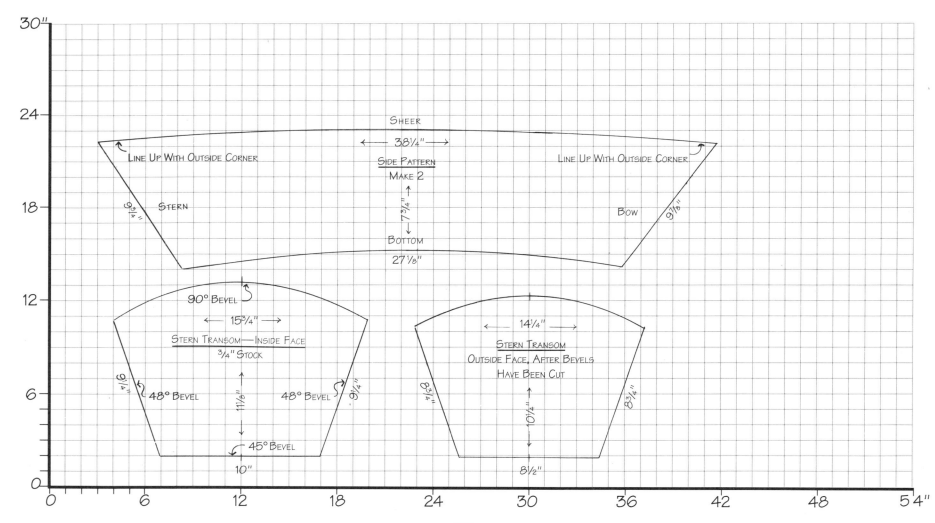

SHEER

← 38¼" →

Line Up With Outside Corner

SIDE PATTERN
MAKE 2

Line Up With Outside Corner

9¾"

STERN

↕ 7¾"

BOW

9⅞"

BOTTOM

27⅛"

90° BEVEL

← 15¾" →

STERN TRANSOM—INSIDE FACE
¾" STOCK

← 14¼" →

STERN TRANSOM
OUTSIDE FACE, AFTER BEVELS
HAVE BEEN CUT

9¼"

48° BEVEL

48° BEVEL

9¼"

8¾"

↕ 11⅛"

↕ 10¼"

8¾"

45° BEVEL

10"

8½"

CRADLE PRAM—"WAVE" ROCKER AND BOW TRANSOM PATTERNS

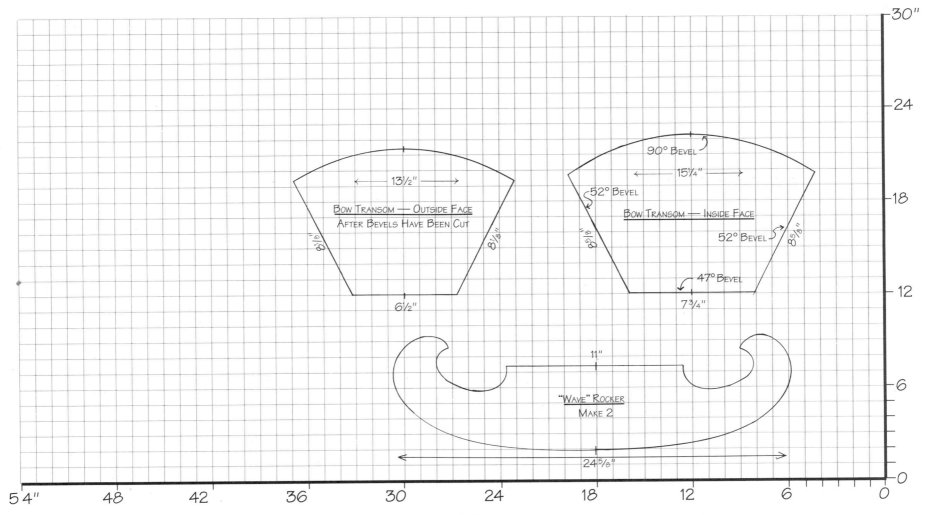

Bow Transom — Outside Face
After Bevels Have Been Cut

13½"

8⅛"

8⅛"

6½"

90° Bevel

15¼"

52° Bevel

Bow Transom — Inside Face

52° Bevel

8⅝"

8⅝"

47° Bevel

7¾"

11"

"Wave" Rocker
Make 2

24⅝"

30"

24

18

12

6

0

54"   48   42   36   30   24   18   12   6   0

Bahama Dinghy—Keel, Stem, Breasthook, Knee, and Mold Patterns

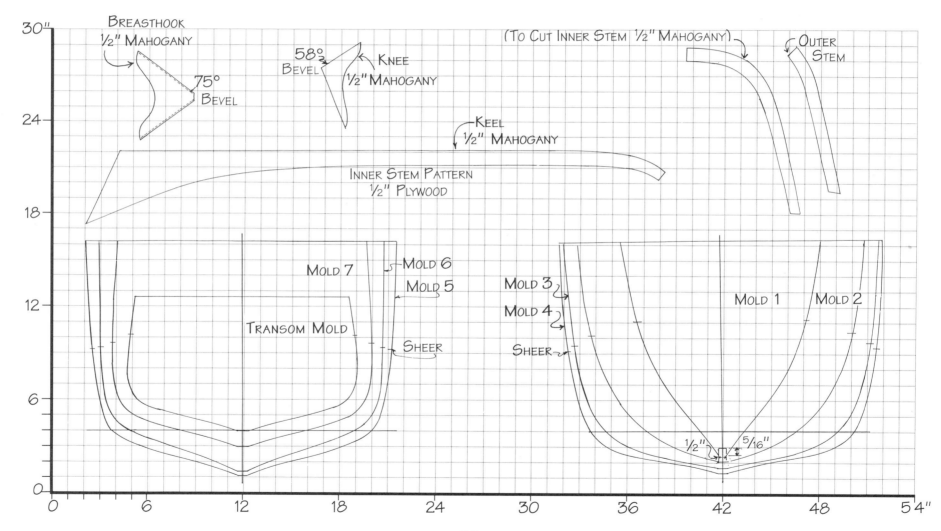

Breasthook
½" Mahogany

75° Bevel

58° Bevel

Knee
½" Mahogany

(To Cut Inner Stem ½" Mahogany)

Outer Stem

Keel
½" Mahogany

Inner Stem Pattern
½" Plywood

Mold 7

Mold 6

Mold 5

Transom Mold

Sheer

Mold 3

Mold 4

Sheer

Mold 1

Mold 2

½"

⁵⁄₁₆"

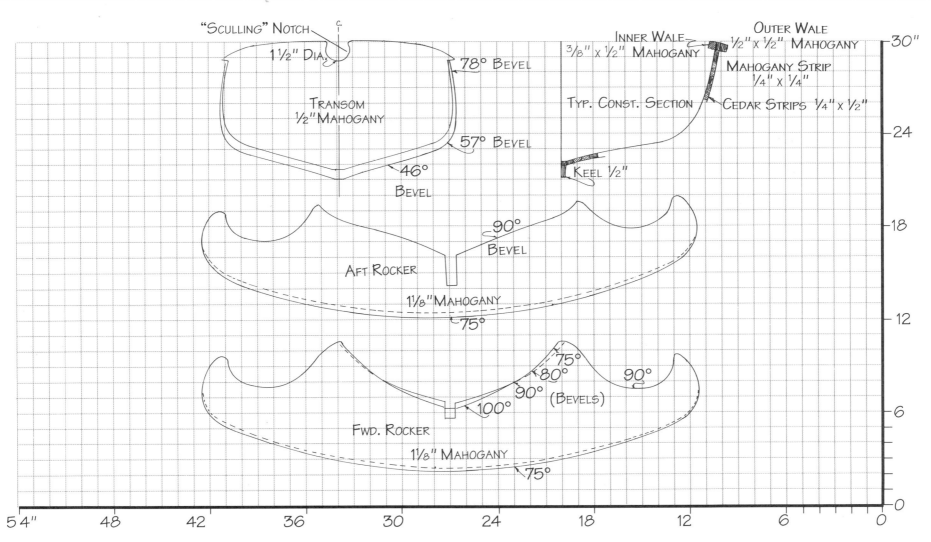

"Sculling" Notch

1½" Dia.

Transom ½" Mahogany

78° Bevel

57° Bevel

46° Bevel

Inner Wale ⅜" x ½" Mahogany

Outer Wale ½" x ½" Mahogany

Mahogany Strip ¼" x ¼"

Typ. Const. Section

Cedar Strips ¼" x ½"

Keel ½"

Aft Rocker

90° Bevel

1⅛" Mahogany

75°

Fwd. Rocker

75°
80°
90°
90°
100°
(Bevels)

1⅛" Mahogany

75°

54"   48   42   36   30   24   18   12   6   0

30"   24   18   12   6   0

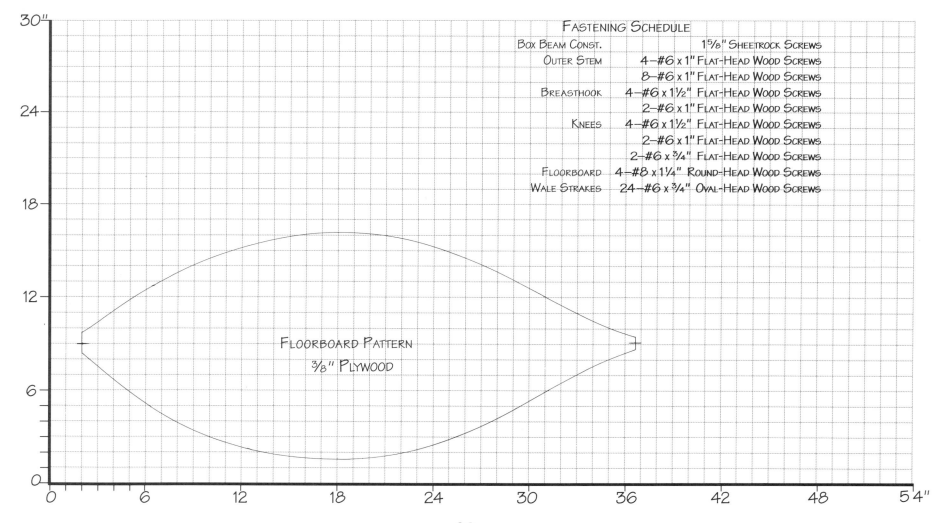

FASTENING SCHEDULE

Box Beam Const.	1⅝" Sheetrock Screws
Outer Stem	4—#6 x 1" Flat-Head Wood Screws
	8—#6 x 1" Flat-Head Wood Screws
Breasthook	4—#6 x 1½" Flat-Head Wood Screws
	2—#6 x 1" Flat-Head Wood Screws
Knees	4—#6 x 1½" Flat-Head Wood Screws
	2—#6 x 1" Flat-Head Wood Screws
	2—#6 x ¾" Flat-Head Wood Screws
Floorboard	4—#8 x 1¼" Round-Head Wood Screws
Wale Strakes	24—#6 x ¾" Oval-Head Wood Screws

Floorboard Pattern

⅜" Plywood

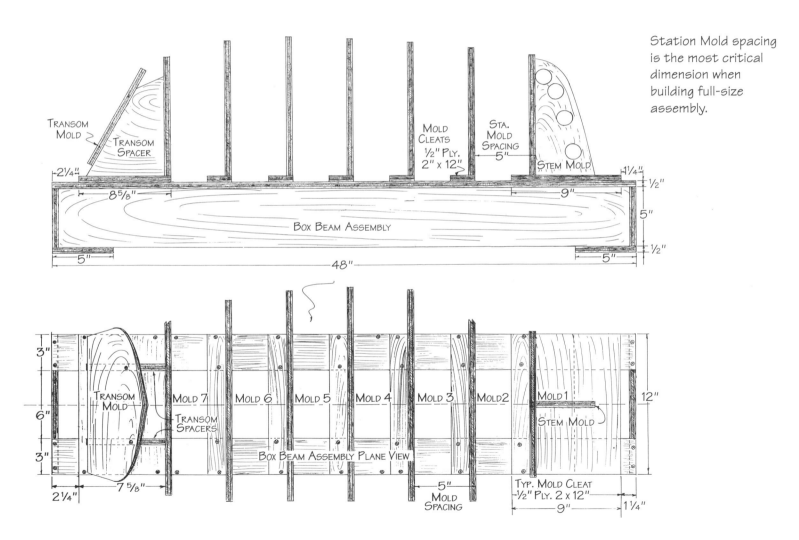

Station Mold spacing is the most critical dimension when building full-size assembly.

Transom Mold

Transom Spacer

Mold Cleats ½" Ply. 2" x 12"

Sta. Mold Spacing 5"

Stem Mold

2¼"

8⅝"

1¼"

½"

5"

½"

Box Beam Assembly

5"

48"

5"

3"

Transom Mold

Mold 7

Mold 6

Mold 5

Mold 4

Mold 3

Mold 2

Mold 1

12"

6"

Transom Spacers

Stem Mold

3"

Box Beam Assembly Plane View

5" Mold Spacing

Typ. Mold Cleat ½" Ply. 2 x 12"

2¼"

7⅝"

9"

1¼"

ACKNOWLEDGMENTS

Our thanks to all who have assisted in this book, especially: Jon Wilson, of WoodenBoat, for his enthusiasm and support; Dick Gorski, for his patience, persistence, and design expertise; Jane Crosen, for her editing, and for her work in the coordination and development of the illustrations; Olga Lange, for her diligent assistance in design and production; and Barbara Bennett, for her commitment to well-printed books.

Buck Smith built a wonderful prototype cradle pram, and H. H. "Dynamite" Payson and Peter Spectre built a variation on it. Bob Lincoln of RKL Boatworks built the prototype Bahama dinghy cradle, and he, Mike O'Brien, and Ted Hugger provided technical advice throughout the project. Many individuals lent encouragement for the idea with their photographs, and their enthusiasm. We are grateful to all.

Buck Smith
Green's Island, Maine

Peter H. Spectre
Camden, Maine

ABOUT THE AUTHOR AND ILLUSTRATOR

PETER H. SPECTRE is a writer and editor who specializes in nautical subjects. He has been an editor with the Naval Institute Press, International Marine Publishing Company, and WoodenBoat Publications. He has written for such magazines as WoodenBoat, Nautical Quarterly, Down East, Le Chasse-Marée, National Fisherman, Small Boat Journal, and others. With George Putz, he edited the seven-volume cult classic, The Mariner's Catalog. With Steven Lang, he wrote On the Hawser: A Tugboat Album. By himself, he wrote Different Waterfronts: Stories from the Wooden Boat Revival. When he isn't locked in combat with the written nautical word, he is rowing, paddling, poling, and sailing his way toward his version of watery Paradise.

That's the boat department. Mr. Spectre is just as adept in the baby department, being a father three times over. Though his children are now grown up, he still claims enough residual knowledge of diapers, safety pins, bottles, etc., to carry him successfully through grandchildren, great-grandchildren, and anything else in a baby way to come along. Mr. Spectre lives in Camden, Maine, with his wife Eileen—and a bunch of old boats.

Because BUCKLEY SMITH is a self-taught artist, his works are unique, often fanciful creations born from his imagination and his passion for boats. Buck began dreaming of boats as a boy, and built wooden models with his father. The graceful lines of boats emerged naturally from his hands, and at the age of twenty Buck began selling his pen-and-ink drawings. Buck then built himself a full-sized sailboat, God's Bread, on which he traveled the world for ten years.

Buck is not only a fine artist whose pen-and-ink sketches are always in demand, but a creative woodworker as well. His designs flow easily from paper to two- and three-dimensional wood pieces, emerging as carvings, sculpture, and hand-made homes. His patented children's rocking-boat design, the Gloucester Rocker, is sold internationally. The Nantucket Whaling Museum commissioned Buck to build a special lapstrake model, now on permanent display.

Based in Morro Bay, California, Buck and his family—wife Becky and sons Brady and Bowen—spend each summer on Green's Island, Maine. They enjoy sailing on their scow sloop Banjo, recently built by Buck and friends and used to ferry everything from people to lumber around Penobscot Bay.